# The Psychology of Reti

# The Psychology of Retirement

## Coping with the Transition from Work

### Derek Milne

*BSc, MSc, DipClinPsych, PhD, CPsychol
(Clinical; Sport and Exercise), FBPsS*

A John Wiley & Sons, Ltd., Publication

Wiley-Blackwell is an imprint of John Wiley & Sons, formed by the merger of Wiley's global Scientific, Technical and Medical business with Blackwell Publishing.

*Registered Office*
John Wiley & Sons Ltd, The Atrium, Southern Gate, Chichester, West Sussex, PO19 8SQ, UK

*Editorial Offices*
350 Main Street, Malden, MA 02148-5020, USA
9600 Garsington Road, Oxford, OX4 2DQ, UK
The Atrium, Southern Gate, Chichester, West Sussex, PO19 8SQ, UK

For details of our global editorial offices, for customer services, and for information about how to apply for permission to reuse the copyright material in this book please see our website at www.wiley.com/wiley-blackwell.

*Library of Congress Cataloging-in-Publication Data*

Milne, D. (Derek)
   The Psychology of Retirement : Coping with the Transition from Work / Derek Milne, BSc, Msc, DipClinPsych, PhD, CPsychol (Clinical; Sport and Exercise), FBPsS.
      pages cm
   Includes bibliographical references and index.
      ISBN 978-0-470-97266-3 (pbk.)
   1. Retirement–Psychological aspects.
   HQ1062.M5495 2013
   155.67′2–dc23

                                                                                        2012029608

A catalogue record for this book is available from the British Library.

Cover image: © thislife pictures / Alamy
Cover design by Design Deluxe

Typeset in 10.5/13pt Minion by Aptara Inc., New Delhi, India
Printed in Singapore by Ho Printing Singapore Pte Ltd

1   2013

For Jan, princess of my heart

# Contents

# About this Book and Author

There are many books on retirement, but this is the first to draw thoroughly on psychology, being the most relevant discipline for formulating the challenge of coping with the transition to retirement. In order to illuminate retirement through psychology, this book applies well-established theories, recent research evidence, retired peoples' personal experiences (in case study format), filtered through my own professional understanding of what helps us to develop through life, based on my work as a Clinical Psychologist with adults in Britain's National Health Service over the past 33 years. I also retired myself a couple of years ago, so have a personal perspective. Work on fostering human development with athletes, coaches, and university students is a further source of guidance.

Based on these foundations, this book provides a primer on coping with retirement by highlighting core issues and challenges, identifying positives, suggesting options, and encouraging an optimistic and constructive approach to this vital transition, complementing the traditional emphasis on the physical and financial aspects of retirement. These aspects of retirement are captured with a RECIPE for addressing this major and rather special transition:

Resources
Exercise
Coping strategies
Intellectual activity
Purpose
Engagement (social support)

Unlike earlier transitions, retirement offers a golden period that starts when working life ends. It is golden because it represents a long-awaited opportunity to develop particular talents and interests, free from the draining demands of work. It is also golden because the time and talent are there, as never before.

# Acknowledgments

I am much indebted to the many people who have encouraged and supported me during the preparation of this book during 2011–12. Many of them have taken the trouble to read draft chapters and to offer suggestions, helping me to improve the flow or richness of the material. Others have simply allowed me to outline my thinking and have offered their valuable reactions. In particular, I am hugely indebted to my partner, Jan Little, for her patient and skilful work on improving the book's flow and coherence, not to mention her general interest and unstinting encouragement. Duncan Gray also deserves a special mention for sharing an unflagging interest in the book's development, and for his stimulating thoughts (e.g. on happiness and money). Similarly, my "case study" contributors should be applauded for telling me about their retirement experiences, warts and all. Within the book they have pseudonyms, and some non-essential details (as far as the book is concerned) have been changed, to protect their anonymity. But to give them the credit that they merit, here are their real names: David Blackwell, Margaret Clark, Lynn and John Joyce, Celia and Jim Keegan, Kevin Robson, Tom Smith, Douglas Thomson, and Keith Turner. Priceless assistance with typing my taped material was provided by Karen Clark and Barbara Mellors at Newcastle University. Graphic artist Angela Butler produced the figures. Research Assistant Laura Maddison searched the scientific literature for relevant studies, helped by Annabel Boon. Valuable feedback on draft material was kindly provided by: Christina Blackwell, Kath Bland, Nichola Burns, Jessica Chapman, Pam Durkin, Ian James, Kath Muat, Roger Paxton, and by all of my case study participants. Interesting ideas and general support was gratefully received from Kirsty Maddison, Alec Milne, and my golfing buddies (Joe Convery, Joe Dickinson, Rob Pratt, Neil Robson, and Alan Watson).

# 1

# The Surprises of Retirement

Retirement: is this our final act, the dimming of the light, the inescapable descent into hopeless senility? The traditional answer is an emphatic "yes," as indicated by the dictionary definition: "To give up, to go away, to seek seclusion, recede or disappear." But recent decades have seen a transformation in the possibilities that are ushered in by retirement, at least in Western society. Improvements in life expectancy mean that, for most of us, there will typically be 15–20 years available for quality living before we truly recede. This is reflected in a review by Baltes in the *American Psychologist*:

> During the last decade, we have witnessed a growing success story regarding young old age. Because of medical, technical, social, economic and educational advances, the overall ... life for 60- and 70-year olds has made major strides in indicators of health and psychological functioning. For this period of the third age, cultural and social forces in industrialized countries have been able to offset, for the most part and for most individuals, the weaknesses inherent in the biological life-span.[1]

In writing this review, Baltes credited the Roman philosopher and statesman Cicero (106–43 BCE) as being the original champion of retirement. Cicero wrote an essay on old age in his early sixties, arguing that a properly-managed retirement provided opportunities for continued personal development. Drawing on Stoicism, he particularly emphasized that the waning interest in "bodily pleasures" removed a major distraction from self-actualization: "Nothing is more directly destructive to the dignity of man than the pursuit of bodily pleasure."[2]

*The Psychology of Retirement: Coping with the Transition from Work*, First Edition. By D. Milne.
© 2013 D. Milne. Published 2013 by John Wiley & Sons, Ltd.

Therefore, a new dawn beckons in our "young old age," and a better current definition might be: *To recede from working life and make a transition to a new life phase, one where new opportunities for happiness and personal development beckon.* On this more optimistic definition, the challenge becomes one of ensuring that we make the most of our final major opportunity to make our life as successful as possible. The idea of making a transition between different phases of our lives (e.g. from adolescent to adult) originates from research on topics like bereavement and other kinds of trauma, though it also applies to seemingly positive changes, like retirement. There appears to be a fairly typical pattern, which starts with emotional turbulence. In the case of retirement, this might include excitement and a "honeymoon period"; in the case of trauma it is more likely to feature numbness, anger, disbelief, and denial. After three or four months there may be some change (similar in both the "positive" and traumatic situations), including confusion, a loss of confidence, and depression. However, if the transition follows a "normal" pattern of adjustment, then over the following three months or so we should see growing acceptance, more exploration of ways forward (e.g. developing a social hobby in retirement), a return of confidence and a changed, more adaptive engagement with everyday life.

The transition into retirement, however, can be surprisingly hard to define: many continue to "work" in various senses of the word, and resuming some form of paid employment after retiring from a career post is common (surveys in the US suggest that over 60 percent of retirees "un-retire" and continue in some form of paid work, then "re-retire" or "semi-retire" some time later). In this sense, experts suggest that initial retirement is not so much the end of one's working life as the beginning of a new stage of working (e.g. the "encore" career). While this used to be restricted to those whose work was necessarily time-limited thereby creating a clear financial need to start a second career (e.g. among athletes), in recent decades this has become something of the norm. In this sense, there is often no single event that delineates retirement completely satisfactorily: it is more like a process that unfolds over a period of years. Factors such as work opportunities, fluctuating finances, personal needs, stages of adjustment, caring for dependant relatives, and other emerging retirement issues all affect this new period of one's life. Experts therefore tend to define retirement as a developmental process; a transition triggered by stopping one's working life and accessing a state pension or a retirement package, but a process that is best defined by the individual and subject to the very different ways that individuals adapt to their particular circumstances and cultures. For example, I have recently ceased working full-time and have taken a retirement package, a single event that for me marked my retirement, but I continue to work for money in ways that used to be part of my job, like writing this book. My transition might be delayed or never truly happen, were I to write books for the rest of my life. Therefore, in a psychological sense I may never fully retire. This book explores whether that is a "cunning plan" or mere denial.

Although an elusive concept, retirement represents a challenge that is facing governments and a growing proportion of the population as the "baby-boomers" reach their sixties, death rates are reduced due to enhanced healthcare, life expectancy increases, and healthier living yields widespread benefits. To illustrate the point about life expectancy, scientists reviewing "anti-aging medicine" describe rapid progress in modifying the aging process, through earlier and better detection of disease, stem cell developments, gene-based therapies, cloning, nanotechnology, and artificial intelligence. Experts believe that future therapies may significantly extend longevity, to the extent that a significant proportion of the population could be enabled to live to 100.

It is also an unprecedented and relatively recent challenge to governments, healthcare providers, pension systems, and many others. The situation was different under Chancellor Otto von Bismarck, when in 1889 Germany became the first country to introduce a social insurance system for those reaching 70 (though even by 1916 the retirement age had reduced to 65). As the relative numbers were small, the governments of the time felt that a mandatory retirement age was appropriate. Since 2000, the position has shifted from "pro-retirement" to "pro-work", in the sense of encouraging older workers to continue to work, with a minimum age set for accessing a deferred pension scheme. In the US in 2010, for instance, there were no longer earning limits for retirees between 65 and 70, thus providing an incentive to continue working, while the age at which security benefits were accessible slowly increased from 65 to 67. Furthermore, the financial crises arising initially in 2008 will have heightened the motivation to continue working for those whose reduced retirement savings and loss of pension benefits were created by the banking collapse.

In this context it is unfortunate (for governments) that there are yet more retirees to consider. "Never in the history of humanity have so many people grown so old at the same time ... an unprecedented aging boom, which will more than double the number of people over 65 by 2050,"[3] so began a piece in the American magazine *Monitor on Psychology*. The article went on to tease out the implications for society. In Britain, this boom was referred to dramatically as "The population time-bomb,"[4] where it was emphasized that for the first time there were at that stage more pensioners than under-16 year-olds. Quoting the Office for National Statistics, the newspaper went on to note a shift from 15 percent of the population being of pensionable age in 1971 to 19 percent in 2008, when the figure had increased at double the previous rate. Although the most marked increase was for the over-eighties, there was a concern about the "explosive" consequences for Britain's National Health Service (NHS) and for pensions. Bear in mind that, when the first pensions were introduced in Britain in 1908, a man of 65 could only expect to live for 12 more years on average, a position that had hardly altered 50 years ago. Now we understand that between 2006 and 2072 the number of people over 65 will double (and those over 80 will treble), resulting in further impacts on the economy and on the NHS (e.g. roughly one-third of mental health services are concerned with the over-sixty-fives).[5] In turn, nearly a fifth of those alive in Britain in 2011 will reach 100.

The statistics from the US are similarly stunning. When the Social Security Act of 1935 first provided benefits to workers reaching the age of 65, the average life expectancy was a mere 62 years, so only a minority actually benefitted. The creation of a formal retirement status appears to have been the US government's response to the Great Depression, as there were very few jobs available. In this context, the older workers needed to be encouraged to give up their jobs for younger workers, hence the introduction of pension plans, mandatory retirement, and so forth. Latterly the prospects for US retirees have become much brighter. For example, someone who was aged 65 in 2007 could expect to live to 74. In terms of the challenge facing US society, the baby boom cohort (i.e. those born between 1946 and 1964) equates to some 78 million people, and they will be reaching their retirement age during the next decade, when their life expectancy will increase yet further. This raises questions about the country's ability to provide a viable retirement income, and experts anticipate that individuals will have to bear more of the financial burden. This is stressful enough, but is aggravated by the individual having to make investment decisions that would previously have been made by the state, as well as having to manage their funds and cope with the associated risk.

These statistics amount to the general position that most of us living in developed countries can currently expect to spend up to a third of our lives in retirement (though such are the concerns for the economy that governments are currently seeking to raise the retirement age, and to remove the obligation on employers and workers to retire at a certain age). In summary, given the major improvements in life expectancy and healthcare, living well into your retirement years has rarely looked so favorable. In turn, this raises questions about how those who retire can make the most of their seeming good fortune: how can we achieve happiness in the newly-protracted era of retirement?

As many have discovered, reaching a contented retirement state it is not necessarily a straightforward or simple matter: estimates suggest that as approximately one-quarter of those who retire will endure a stressful, complicated transition. This is partly due to health problems, as one's sixties is a time when illness strikes. According to The Office for National Statistics, in the UK a man can, on average, enjoy good health until 63, whereupon he can expect to suffer a limiting illness for another 15 years before dying. Women do better, suffering a significant illness at 65 and living until they are 82. In the US, the National Center for Health Statistics was more specific about the average onset of diseases for men and women combined: diabetes at 51, arthritis at 55, breast cancer at 61, prostate cancer at 68, and rectal cancer at 71! A pretty sobering set of statistics and part of the reason for regarding retirement as challenging, while also recognizing that there are now treatments that can limit or even remove most of these diseases. As a result, the period that someone of 60 can now expect to remain "unlimited" by illness (i.e. able to function with limited discomfort or limited disability) in Western countries is increasing, almost by the year (one expert estimated that life expectancy was increasing currently by 2.5 years every decade). This is increasing the "wellness window," giving us increasing years to develop through retirement.

Chronic illness is not the only threat facing retirees, as there is also a psychological challenge. This arises (as it does for every other transition we have to make through our lives) because we reach another threshold in our development; another milestone or "turning point" when we need to take stock and adapt to changing circumstances and fresh tasks. A classic instance is coping with retirement from paid employment. The case study of Trevor in this chapter is an illustration. Indeed, the main inspiration for writing this book was to highlight and try to address the surprisingly tricky experience that many face on retirement. To treat the transition with the care and attention it merits, I have set out a "recipe" for success. This is drawn from the latest research, from relevant theories of human development, and from general wisdom on how we might best cope (i.e. what my sample of case studies have to say about succeeding, together with my own experience as a clinical psychologist). Of course, there are numerous ingredients in successful coping during retirement, but the basic ones can be set out in this acronym:

**R**esources (e.g. sufficient money)
**E**xercise
**C**oping strategies
**I**ntellectual activity
**P**urpose
**E**ngagement (social support)

Some of these basic ingredients are more significant than others, more powerful or central in their importance, and so this book will naturally give due weight to them. Prime among the basic ingredients is the way that we cope, the social and psychological strategies that we are able to draw on to tackle the challenges we face in developing. The RECIPE acronym also helps us to think about how the ingredients are combined – what are the accompanying instructions for a successful retirement? In this sense one might say that we should start with the act of retirement, a significant life event. What is the particular nature of that momentous event? Next we should attend to the way that it was processed – was it whisked up into something that became overwhelming? This is the matter of "appraisal", the way that we interpret what is happening. If we happen to perceive our retirement as momentous, we might gear ourselves up for a monstrous struggle, but at the cost of burning up excessive energy. This process of appraisal then triggers our initial coping strategy ("how do I deal with this situation?"), and there is a fair chance that it will be something to do with avoiding or escaping from an uncomfortable situation, as these strategies appear to be the most popular. If this works, then we will tend to busy ourselves with the next problem we face. And so it continues: rarely do we pause for some thoughtful, balanced re-appraisal of what we faced, or of how we faced it. In so doing, we will have missed the chance to develop how we tackle life's challenges. One of the features of retirement is that we have a special opportunity to reflect constructively on our life, special because we now know better than ever that we should be making the most of our situation, probably have better resources for coping than ever before ("life wisdom"), and perhaps too an enhanced realization that "this is it": this could well be our final transition, so let's give it our best shot!

## Stress and Retirement

Although surveys suggest that the majority of retirees feel comfortable about their retirement these days (reporting happiness, emotional wellbeing, and life satisfaction), it was not long ago that the situation was rather different. For instance, prior to World War II retirement was uncommon, partly because life expectancy was much lower, but also because there was no state mandate or pension provision. However, the international advent of compulsory and pensioned retirement has not been straightforward. Although the majority do experience positive reactions, for others there are disturbing mental health problems (e.g. depression and loneliness). In those early days, retirement was new and judged by some experts at that time as being "highly stressful" to the whole population. For example, research from the 1970s noted the stressful experience of alienation, exaggerated by the limited social expectations or roles for retirees, but the stress reported at that time was generally reduced to a more moderate level. And when these people took on "shadow work" (i.e. unpaid but valued social duties) such as child care (grandparenting), caring for disabled spouses or peers, and acting as volunteers the situation improved, no doubt aided by changing social attitudes to this emergent status of "retired."

To be specific, around the 1970s Western experts estimated that about 30 percent of retirees encountered psychological problems, leading some to talk of the "retirement disease." More sophisticated recent research suggests a more extensive spectrum of distress, but no evidence of a disease. To illustrate, at the turn of the millennium one study drew representative samples from the US Health and Retirement Study and followed them over an eight-year period. It was found that about 70 percent of retirees experienced little or no psychological discomfort, while 25 percent reported clear negative consequences: ambivalence, anxiety, fear, depression, and feelings of loss and uselessness (but these were temporary and improved with time). The remaining 5 percent experienced positive changes. So, although the transition to retirement appears to have become less stressful for most people latterly, there is still some significant stress to be addressed or endured, as reflected in reports of retirement as "the knock-out blow," including "health shocks" aggravated by factors like insufficient money or an enforced retirement.

## About this Book

This book attempts to aid the process of addressing the stress of retiring for the significant minority of the population who struggle to make the adjustment, especially in the acute adjustment window of one or two years following retirement, and where mild-to-moderate distress or difficulty is experienced (although the material is also relevant to those who are doing well, or who simply seek a better grasp of what is happening to themselves or a loved one). Rather than viewing this adjustment process as a disease, the book explains what is happening psychologically, and by details strategies for coping successfully with the retirement challenge.

As already illustrated, I will be drawing on psychology for my inspiration, in the shape of well-established theories, the best available research evidence, some retired people's comments on their experience (the "case studies"), and my own professional understanding of what helps us to tick, based on 33 years' work as a Clinical Psychologist with adults. I also retired myself a couple of years ago, so bring a personal perspective. I intend that this book will provide a primer on coping with retirement, by highlighting core issues and challenges, identifying positives, suggesting options, and encouraging an optimistic and constructive approach to this vital transition which, it is hoped, will complement the traditional emphasis on the physical and financial aspects of retirement. Some might say that this psychological perspective is somewhat overdue. However, it would be misleading to indicate that there is a wealth of evidence on which to draw. To illustrate, reviews of research in 2011 published in the scientific journal *American Psychologist* emphasize how little we know about some basic issues. For instance, we do not know much about how involuntary retirement (e.g. redundancy, ill-health) impacts on adjustment over time, and the authors were only able to identify one scientific study about the (demonstrated) effectiveness of preretirement planning or counseling. Similarly, they could point to very little research on the benefits (or otherwise) of popular self-help strategies, designed to foster adjustment in retirement. However, they were sanguine about the latter, as these strategies are based on established methods from clinical and counseling psychology. Therefore, we are in a position of having limited high-quality scientific information to guide retirement specifically, but much more research of general relevance to the adult population. Also, we can refer to some established psychological theories about human development, consider expert consensus, and draw on case studies about many other practical issues. This book will adopt this strategy to offer the best available evidence on how to cope successfully with retirement.

The book aims to foster your maturing process in order to help you to achieve your potential and to secure personal happiness. A further feature of this book is to encourage you to try out some of the ideas, to become something of a "personal scientist," seeking through trial and error to understand how you can be the best you can possibly be. In the past, being at work may well have provided the impetus and framework for this development, but for many the onus is now more personal – developing on through retirement falls squarely on your shoulders this time!

There will be much more on the ingredients for the retirement RECIPE in the chapters that follow, but first I want to give some personal "color" to the retirement issues highlighted in my first case study, "Trevor" and will draw out the main issues raised. (Please note: all case study names are pseudonyms.)

## "Trevor": A Case Study of Retirement as a Trauma

Trevor's background was in the construction industry, where he had set up his first business at the age of 27. Trevor relished operating as an entrepreneur, and by the time he was 53 he was financially able to retire. At this time Trevor was aware that his energy levels were beginning to decline, the work had always been challenging in a difficult, demanding industry and the offer to sell up felt at the time "like a pension scheme." Therefore, unlike the majority who gradually work towards retirement, Trevor "retired suddenly," receiving an offer for his business out of the blue and perceiving it as a "Godsend."

### How Did He Appraise His Situation?

Trevor's first reaction to retirement was one of relief: "felt responsibility stripping away from me"; he had a real sense of achievement, referring to himself as "you lucky bxxxxxd." There was a major "sense of achievement, pure Maslow," as he felt he had entered a "personal fiefdom," a highly acceptable world in which his dislike of taking orders or being within a rigid workplace was satisfied: he felt he'd been born an entrepreneur. When things became more difficult (e.g. a relationship problem, as described below) during his early retirement he took the view that he should grapple with and ultimately manage these challenges, just as he'd always done within his work. An entrepreneur to the end, he believed that, "like Kipling, if you could treat triumph and disaster the same" then you were doing well. Trevor's view of events was strongly influenced by the notion of stages of development, in particular the view that one "shouldn't hanker back" but should try to treat stressful events as an opportunity for further development. In this way we can better meet our need for esteem and self-actualization, ideally in fresh ways. Appropriately enough for an entrepreneur, Trevor saw the need to re-invent himself, and so he drew an explicit analogy between his predicament and the metamorphosis of the butterfly. He viewed retirement as causing him to problem-solve, using his experience and intelligence to flex his new set of wings.

### Which Stressors were Present?

"Retirement is half the money and twice the husband" was a heartfelt quote offered by Trevor: when he reached the age of 53 he divorced his second wife due to her problems with alcohol. Later that year, his first wife died, at the age of only 52. She was the mother of his children, and Trevor had been estranged for 15 years from her (and their children) before he met his second wife.

Trevor's second marriage followed a period of living together. However, within three years they had divorced, a "terrible catastrophe". This three-year period coincided with the sale of his business. Trevor felt that the divorce was partly due to her history (she'd already been married twice before), but largely due to changes he felt were occurring within himself, due to giving up the business. This represented a huge "double whammy," coming as it did on the back of losing his business and presenting him with a prolonged task of adjustment. According to Trevor's mother, still alive and a major source of support, she felt "you still haven't got through it," even at the time of our interview, several years later.

### How Did He Cope?

Due to the above, Trevor found the initial six weeks of retirement to be a very traumatic period. He thought that he went through "denial and shock . . . a

**Figure 1.1**　Trevor's retirement challenge was to piece together his new life, like a jigsaw puzzle

bereavement thing, including an unreal experience ... seriously traumatic." Trevor felt that he had: "lost his identity ... his role as an entrepreneur."

To try to cope with this uncomfortable state, he drew the analogy with "having to make a new jigsaw up," one in which he represented the central pieces and where new surrounding pieces had to be found and inserted, so that his life could form a coherent picture again (see Figure 1.1).

At the age of 51 he had achieved what he regarded as the zenith of his business career, gaining an MBA at a prestigious local university. Now in this traumatic period he considered that extending this academic activity might represent one of the vital pieces in his jigsaw. In true entrepreneurial tradition, he contacted the business school in which he had obtained a 1st and "grovelled for a job." Given his business experience and his previous academic excellence, he was invited to teach a course and to be the Senior

Research Assistant leading a nationally-funded project concerned with the management of key relationships in small businesses.

Characteristically, Trevor didn't stop there, adding consultancy and teacher training to the pieces of the jigsaw. After a while he "found (his) feet ... playing my cards as best as I could ... re-shaping life as best as I could." In the same vein, having discovered that he could teach, he went on to train as a vocational teacher, gaining several NVQ awards after the age of 60 and some three to four years after his initial retirement. He even became quite enthusiastic about the NVQ awards, which allowed him to gain additional higher qualifications, adding them "like a boy scout" collecting badges.

## Trevor's Personality

Trevor felt that much of his experience of retirement could be understood better through realizing that he'd been an only child "equipped to be self-contained, something of an island." His character determined that, when facing the kinds of traumatic, turbulent experiences that retirement brought for him, "enough is enough ... get on with doing something about it." For him this meant writing a book related to his work and getting involved in his professional association, in addition to the other coping adjustments already noted. He was also committed to being a lifelong learner and loved his books: within his view of the world: "time is the greatest gift of retirement ... one should treat the threats seriously but have time for oneself, something that is very healing."

## Social Support

Trevor noted that, in the role of boss, one needs to be "peculiarly equipped" to cope with social relationships, as the only true peers with whom one can relate normally are other businessmen. Even with them it is "part of the animal to keep your cards close to your chest ... always "doing fine." Whereas retirement for some people means a time of greater intimacy and enhanced satisfaction with existing relationships, in Trevor's case the opposite happened: having had one marriage disintegrate, he had also rather quickly lost a second wife, something for which he assumed responsibility: "I wasn't the man she married ... a confident businessman." Interestingly, when asked about the support that he'd received from others, Trevor recounted examples of where he had been the one providing the support. However, there were some clear-cut examples of Trevor engaging in activities that provided him with different kinds of support, such as being a singer with the local choir. Although this was tinged with some negatives, it did provide him with a satisfying social activity.

At the time of our interview (some eight years after his retirement), Trevor's social support included:

- *Emotional support:* Trevor appeared to me to find this topic difficult to discuss: he couldn't readily identify his own negative feelings, or list people who provided emotional support to him. The exception was his mother, whom he perceived to be "mature and clear- thinking," someone who was a real help. Trevor had been "programmed to be a provider," so when he lost his job he "lost his role." Indeed, the theme of bereavement and loss seems to have been the dominant emotional impact of his retirement, and there still appeared to be a gulf where his emotional support should be. This is perhaps is one of the missing pieces of his jigsaw.

  Trevor also has some negative emotions, especially disliking "well-meaning but seriously patronizing and stereotyping people ... there is no need to feel sorry for old people" due to thinking about his own aging process, how he feels at his present age, and especially through watching how his mother has dealt with aging. This challenged his view that old age was something to feel sorry about. Although he believes that such a view is widespread (he shared it too), he has come to realize that old age is "not a pitiable thing. It can be full and peaceful, even through the physical deterioration."

- *Informational support:* This was a more comfortable topic for Trevor to discuss, perhaps as it was closer to his skills as an entrepreneur. For him, it was a "network issue ... friends help me to gain an overview or perspective ... stop me getting too close ... provide alternative perspectives." He had actively sought to increase his network and had approached old contacts for academic, teaching, and other useful links to work.

- *Practical support:* A major problem for Trevor was "a double-edged sword ... loss of access to friends who were still in their careers (the other businessmen who hadn't retired) ... and still in their settled relationships." This meant that they couldn't socialize in the same way as someone who was single and retired. However, perhaps because of his personality and entrepreneurial drive, practical help was something that Trevor had little use for: "never needed ... what would you give to a man who has everything? ... can always manage ... never ask for it," though he is far more inclined to give practical support.

- *Companionship*: Although his social network contains relatively few people, perhaps because of Trevor's drive and intellect, he does enjoy getting together with his friends and having a "beer and a chat"; he likes the idea of a "good friend coming out to play." However, Trevor is keenly aware that maintaining such relationships with others who are still working is decidedly problematic, as the relationship can become unequal.

## Understanding Stress

Trevor's stressors are striking examples of how things like our relationships and work experiences can shape the situation in which we find ourselves. It is a common fallacy to assume that such stressors drive how we feel, becoming the focus of our discontent (e.g. a problematic marriage). By contrast, to Trevor's credit he seemed to view his stressors as the signal to do something, to react to improve his situation.

Let us now take a look at the psychology of stress. First a word on definition, which is much needed in relation to the confused concept of "stress." Although the term is usually associated with unpleasant events ("stressed out," "under stress," a "stressful life event," etc.), it is more accurate to view stress as a pressure, something that we feel we have to react to in some way. This can be a "major life event," like moving home, or a subjective experience, like pain: it is whatever we deem worthy of our attention and as meriting a reaction. Stressors in the modern workplace include tight deadlines, periodic re-training, challenging contracts (with the implicit threat of redundancy), and the expectation that employees will work ever-longer hours. It doesn't end there: as retirees, Western society expects us to help care for our grandchildren; provide financial help to our children; and care for our family dependents. Stressors of this kind may lead to "distress" (also called "strain"), the unpleasant consequence of our not coping successfully with a stressor, as in feeling angry or depressed.

Not so long ago, researchers and the general public believed that exposure to stressful life events such as unemployment or marital conflict was the cause of personal dysfunction and distress (e.g. depression). This fuelled the creation of lists of stressful events, ranked from high to low, and an emphasis on stressors in popular writing (e.g. "How losing your partner can make you depressed"). Here are some examples, related to retirement:

- A changed and still rapidly-changing society, where our established values and ways of living may have disappeared altogether, or been severely eroded, causing constant irritation (generation gaps, etc.);
- The death of family members and close friends becomes an increasingly frequent event as we age. In addition, the older we get the more we witness the distress of these close friends who survive. We may even notice with a shiver how celebrities and other well-known individuals are passing on, perhaps at a younger age than our own;
- Health is another sure marker of the passage of time, bringing with it gradually accruing impairments, some of them becoming more serious and disabling over time;
- With these physical and other age-related declines another stressor is our growing inability to sustain a meaningful, purposeful function in life. This function would normally have been achieved through our work, which for some represents a calling or vocation, a deeply satisfying way to make a living and feel fulfilled. After all, work is a powerful, defining phenomenon in society, contributing significantly to our sense of self, our wellbeing, and the feeling of making a useful contribution
- Awareness that one's own death is that step closer, a widely-experienced source of dread, naturally avoided or denied as much as possible. This has a certain inevitability, as we are keenly aware of our past and present, and hence what the future inevitably holds.

However, recent developments in the way we understand stress suggest a much more interactive process of adjustment. Far from there being some kind of fixed relationship between certain life events and distress, it appears that individuals show highly variable reactions to stressors: research indicates that only about 10 percent of distress can be explained by stress. This is because some people remain remarkably healthy and unaffected, despite exposure to quite stressful situations; some are deeply distressed by and "ruminate" on their woes; whereas others appear to mature more rapidly as a result of managing difficult circumstances effectively (i.e. they "transact" with their stressors, making them more manageable). At first researchers thought that these somewhat paradoxical findings were explained by problems within the research itself, such as using faulty instruments to measure peoples' feelings. However, as these queries resolved, researchers began to reduce the emphasis on individual weaknesses and vulnerabilities, emphasizing instead the adaptive strengths and resilience that individuals showed when exposed to difficult circumstances. It was as if we could best understand stress as something that we see as a threat or a challenge, merely the triggering event for what then unfolds, with the outcome heavily influenced by how we cope. Therefore, stress was not best understood as the "cause" of distress, but as something triggering a dynamic process mediated by the way we appraise the stressor, how well we are able to cope, and our social support (as illustrated in Trevor's story). One person's life-threatening stressor was another person's salvation (e.g. divorce): it all seemed to depend on personal qualities such as temperament and life experiences, embedded in our life circumstances or "context." In this sense, stressors merit our serious attention, but it would be a mistake to give specific stressors a particular significance: it all depends on that "transaction" between the individual and the stressor, taking into account the context (including job factors, social support, and economic considerations).

## Appraisals and Assumptions: Making Sense of Stressors

Trevor's retirement experience not only highlights stressors, coping, and distress. It also highlights the critical role played by his perspective – his way of looking at things. An example was the way that he initially viewed his retirement as an achievement. Another is how he later regarded the difficulties he experienced as a challenge, a stimulus to his further development. We call the immediate mental reaction to a stressor an "appraisal," an automatic thought. The first phase in appraisal is to decide if it is a threat, which is quickly followed by an assessment of our ability to cope with the stressor. These appraisals normally happen instantaneously, without conscious thought. An appraisal plays these two critical roles, it represents a kind of mental crossroads, capable of switching on a state of panic or signaling "relax – no need to panic." There then follows a more deliberate period of trying to understand what is happening, and to work out how best to respond. This builds on our fundamental beliefs and the assumptions we make about the situation, both based on our personal experience. The kind of personal values and rules for coping that we have built up over the years will then shape our interpretation (the thinking aspect) and reaction (the feelings that accompany the interpretation, and any behavioral action that we consider necessary).

Researchers and clinicians have tried to identify the kinds of interpretations that are generally made by retired people. As these are the constructions that these people make in their heads, in response to stressors, it is not the stressor itself that is of concern, but rather the view that the individual takes of the stressor. We become upset not so much by what happened, as by what we believe it signifies. As the ancient Greeks recognized (e.g. Epictetus), it is the view that we take of events that makes them challenging, not so much the events themselves: one person's "major life event" is a stimulating transition to another. For example, if we view redundancy as an indication of our personal worth, as a sign that we are useless, we are likely to become distressed. But, if we view it is the opportunity to retire, something that happened for financial reasons affecting the employer, we are likely to feel more positively about the event.

Here are some common examples of important interpretations, drawing on the work of a former colleague, Ellie Stirling:[6]

a.  *Loss of control, autonomy and individuality:* We may no longer be able to achieve our chosen state or goal, even with support, and our choices may be compromised. For instance, we may lack the energy or motivation to stand up for our rights with neighbors. We may well face an unprecedented sense of "not mattering," of being discounted as a "has-been," just another old person.

b.  *Being seen as a financial and social burden:* In the modern world, people may be seen increasingly as commodities, with production as the primary objective of society. This can make retired people feel a burden, particularly those who are unable to contribute in any meaningful way (such as voluntary work).

c.  *Rejection:* This can happen to any group who appears different to others, for reasons such as the way we dress, our age, or our physical mobility. This can lead to the separation and relocation of older people "for their own good," or a process of invalidation in which the views of retired people are discounted, simply because they are retired.

Taken together these kinds of negative interpretations may "destroy peoples' self-esteem, confidence and hope."[7] In the constructive, upbeat spirit of her book and here, I also need to note some of the positive interpretations that may typically accompany retirement:

- The opportunity to undertake work of a different kind: evidence suggests that wellbeing does not decline following retirement, provided that we can find other ways of satisfying our psychological and social needs (for example, replacing paid full-time work with voluntary, part-time work; other ways of supporting our community).
- There can be a huge satisfaction in reaching a successful retirement, as this represents a natural conclusion to an effective and valued working life, not to mention a useful contribution to one's extended family and others. For many, there is the relief of pressure in terms of a stressful job (see Tom's story, in Chapter 6). For others it is the opportunity to undertake all those activities that have been long-awaited, such as a major travelling expedition, or participation in gentle sports such as golf or bowling. At last you are your own boss, free to choose how to spend your time and free to savor activities previously postponed.
- Caring for one's children (and especially one's grandchildren) can be a source of profound joy for many retirees. Indeed, often people will uproot their home to be closer to their extended family, so that they can enjoy more frequent and satisfying contact.
- Relationships with one's partner or other "close confiding others" can evolve, so that they both grow in their appreciation of one another (in the sense that these provide a source of mutual pleasure). This can include reminiscing about important moments in a shared history, or discussing the emotional meanings of ongoing events in a way that inevitably draws on your age, beliefs and experiences.

## The Importance of Coping

What runs through the material above is the idea that stressors can be tackled in ways that can limit their impact, make things worse, or which can even transform them into opportunities for personal development and happiness. How we relate to the stressors is a complex and dynamic process, one that is elastic, capable of taking many different forms, and which can yield diverse outcomes, as illustrated by our appraisals. It is also a transactional process, in the sense that we interact with stressors (and other features of our environment) in ways that can change us and also change that environment. For instance, if we are stressed by our partner's nagging and cope by discussing this constructively, then we may reduce both the nagging and our partner's approach. Coping is the focus of the next chapter, so I will not dwell on it here, except to make the point that it is THE critical psychological factor in determining the success of your retirement transition. It refers to the ways we have of thinking, feeling, and behaving in response to stressors, such as the way that Trevor developed and became a teacher. Coping is the mechanism through which we shape our adjustment to retirement, the main thing that we can seek to control in order to shape our transition. It includes optimizing our development and minimizing losses or declining powers.

Coping may also be maladaptive (harmful), as typically happens when it is based on avoidance or on an emotional preoccupation with something (e.g. regrets over a failed relationship) that one might otherwise deal with actively (e.g. by repairing or replacing that relationship). It is important to recognize that emotion-focused coping like a preoccupation with one's regrets may at times be the most adaptive reaction, particularly when the situation cannot be controlled or when there is nothing that coping can do to improve the situation (e.g. caring for a partner with a severe dementia). Other situations where avoidance-based coping may be appropriate include when there is a lack of understanding about how we could improve matters, or where for personal reasons we are unable to react effectively. These points again emphasize the personal, situational, and transactional nature of coping. This makes general statements problematic, encouraging us to instead look hard at the situation and how our coping efforts are actually working.

With these caveats in mind, what does research indicate about the different coping strategies? There is a wealth of data to suggest that avoidance-based coping is usually associated with either ongoing distress or the development of even more negative consequences (the "vicious cycle": see Chapter 2). Avoidance-based coping includes things like alcohol abuse and reliance on recreational drugs, wishful thinking, escape fantasies, extreme efforts to deny the threat or difficulty, self-distraction, and a basic mental disengagement from the stressors and the challenges. As noted, there are exceptions and some research confirms that not thinking about certain things can be an effective short-term way to cope, as it may provide relief from distress and a way of "getting by" in the short-term (e.g. respite care for a dependent partner). However, the long-term use of avoidance strategies is generally found to be problematic, hence this book presents more active, solution-focused coping strategies.

## How Are You Coping?

As noted, one of the surest ways to assess our coping strategies lies in terms of their observed effectiveness: does their use remove distress? Does it foster wellbeing? Another useful point of reference is in relation to the signs of good mental health. Some examples of good mental health are:

- being able to use your talents and energy productively;
- enjoying challenges and gaining pleasure from accomplishing tasks;
- being capable of sustaining a meaningful love relationship (including genuine intimacy and caring);
- finding meaning in belonging and contributing to your community (e.g. by guiding and nurturing others);
- being responsive, sensitive and empathic to other people's needs and feelings;
- appreciating and responding to humor;
- coming to terms with painful experiences from the past (e.g. finding meaning in them);
- being comfortable and at ease in social situations; energetic and outgoing; and
- being conscientious and responsible.

Reference to this kind of list is a useful benchmark, when reflecting on how we are coping. Useful terms here are "resilience" and "flourishing." The first means coping well despite adversity and hardship, in contrast to being vulnerable, struggling and having poor outcomes (the opposite of the "signs" above). Resilience is thought to come from personal qualities (e.g. intelligence: see below), learning how to cope more effectively, and social support (including learning how to re-interpret events from friends and family). Flourishing refers to a state of enhanced wellbeing resulting from resilience, one in which we can distinguish the experiences of "emotional" wellbeing (e.g. feeling good about coping with a difficult situation), "psychological" wellbeing (e.g. having a sense of mastery or personal growth), and "social" wellbeing (e.g. feeling a sense of belonging and giving to your community).

These thriving states represent successful aging, also called "healthy aging," "aging well," and "productive aging."

## Who are You?

At different points in this chapter I have noted several aspects of our personal make-up, such as temperament and personality. Let's now be a bit more systematic about our make-up. Perhaps the most fundamental building block to recognize is our temperament, a genetically-endowed disposition towards the world that is primarily shaped by early childhood experiences, as in being a calm or excitable person "by nature." Built on this foundation, our personality is the way that we tend to behave, our "character" or the part we play (the term comes from "persona," the mask worn in ancient Greek plays). For instance, "conscientiousness" is a personality trait, one of several ways in which we exercise the vital ability to alter our reactions and overcome stressors. Together with our intelligence, self-control is by far the most important attribute in enabling us to live successful and productive lives, the ability to regulate or change the way we deal with life. Being conscientious means restraining our impulses or substituting one response for another, built on persistence, prudence and organization (see "The Longevity Project," below). It has been called "willpower" and our "moral muscle," and appears especially crucial when we are trying to cope with limited resources. In emphasizing our coping strategies, this book details just how we can apply self-control and intelligence to retirement.

While our temperament tends to be highly stable throughout our lives, our personality can change, though this would usually take a fairly significant life event, like retirement or long-term therapy. More commonly, our personality make-up is an enduring disposition to the world, something that will remain fairly stable, so if we develop into a sociable, dominant extravert in our teens we are likely to be recognizably the same person when we retire. This means that self-awareness is vital, so you can "know yourself" and the kinds of biases and pitfalls to which you are prone. As Robert Burns put it:

O wad some Pow'r the giftae gie us
To see ourselves as others see us!
It wad frae mony a blunder free us
And foolish notion

Books that include personality tests have been developed to enable such insight. To assess personality dimensions like "extraversion," they include questions like: "would you rate yourself as a lively individual?" "Are you likely to be quick and sure in your actions?" and "Do you usually take the initiative in making new friends?" A recent research study illustrates the role of personality in shaping our experience of fun.[8] A questionnaire was given to 1,100 undergraduates studying in London and suggested five different kinds of fun, such as fun in taking risks, spontaneous fun, and fun associated with being with funny people. The researchers then correlated these with a "big five" personality measure (the five factors are: Neuroticism, Extraversion, Openness to Experience, Agreeableness, and Conscientiousness) and other personal characteristics (gender, age, etc.). The authors' concluded that there was a complex relationship:

> for an extravert a party may be the essence of fun, while for a person high on Openness it maybe to a visit a science park, museum or gallery. Thus an agreeable, conscientious, female, middle-aged introvert may have a very different conception of fun from a young, neurotic, poorly-educated, sensation-seeking male ... In this sense fun activities may be defined as those which satisfy various specific psychological needs for the individual. This is why the term is both subjective and multifaceted."[9]

Research suggests some interesting links between personality and coping. The Longevity Project[10] began in 1921 with 1,500 10-year-old children, a group whose development has been followed ever since. The findings (based on life expectancy, work patterns, pet ownership, personal habits, and much more) suggested that the conscientious children in this sample had more stable relationships and so partly helped them to live longer and happier. They were dependable, prudent, persistent types who minimized risks. By contrast, their more impulsive compatriots were more likely to drink, smoke, and eat a poor diet. These gambles with their health shortened their lives. Returning to the idea of retirement as a stimulus for personality change, an American study compared the personalities of a sample of 223 adults who remained in employment versus a comparable group of 144 people who retired. The findings indicated that personality did not predict who would retire, but that those who did retire increased on the personality factor of "agreeableness" and decreased on "activity" (part of extraversion), relative to those who stayed in work. Satisfaction with retirement was highest for those who were low on "neuroticism" and high in "extraversion." After retirement, those research participants described themselves as less active (i.e.

slower-paced and less vigorous) as well as less competitive and argumentative, compared to their working selves. The data led the authors to state that personality was an important part of understanding the retirement experience, and to note that the main personality traits did not change, although there were a couple of significant retirement-related changes in select aspects of extraversion and introversion.

Atop our temperament and personality we can think about some core beliefs (also called "schemas" and "lifetraps") that contribute to the part we play in life. Schemas are mental patterns, a framework for thinking, whether positively or negatively; by contrast, lifetraps are self-defeating (maladaptive) ways of behaving, based on the beliefs one holds about oneself. There are about a dozen common lifetraps, such as "defectiveness" (i.e. I am flawed, so am unlovable and deserve to be rejected); "self-sacrifice"; "approval-seeking," and "entitlement" (i.e. feeling special, superior or important, meaning that rules are things that other people follow). A recent book, *The Narcissism Epidemic*,[11] deals with the "pernicious spread" of the entitlement "plague,"[12] with consequences for us all (a survey of college students indicated that two out of three agreed that their generation was more narcissistic than their predecessors). The authors use narcissism to refer to over-confidence about attractiveness, shallow values, disinterest in close relationships, vanity, and self-admiration. A questionnaire measuring narcissism has items like these: "I like to look at myself in the mirror"; "I get upset when people don't notice how I look"; and "I like to show off my body." In terms of suggesting how we might become better able to minimize our narcissistic tendencies, in addition to heightening self-awareness (fill in the questionnaire, etc.), they advocate strengthening important relationships (i.e. making them more stable and caring), increasing expressions of gratitude, and engaging in personally humbling activities. At the same time, we can weaken interest in the causes (which they attribute to such causes as materialism, parenting, the media, cosmetic surgery, social networking on the Internet, antisocial behavior, and a culture that positively encourages entitlement).

To clarify how these different parts of our make-up combine, consider how an event like redundancy may tap into a personality issue related to feeling defective or second-rate, something that has bubbled around our life since school days, and has led into maladaptive coping. It may have arisen because a teacher was hypercritical, but more often it seems to be due to the way that parents treat their children, as in repeatedly pointing out flaws or undermining personal effectiveness (see, for example,

*Re-Inventing Your Life*[13]). If self-help books such as this do not work, a therapist might help people suffering from this personality disposition by developing their awareness of this pattern and its origins, then proceeding to help them strengthen relevant coping strategies (like their ability to appraise stressors more logically, attributing responsibility where it is due, rather than automatically assuming the blame).

## Putting it All in Context

The transactions that we have with stressors occur in a context filled with social, physical, economic, historical, cultural, and other variables. Retirement is more likely to be a smooth transition if your partner is retiring at the same time, you are both healthy, there are sound pension arrangements in place, and both of you have had a satisfying employment history. Imagine the contrasting prospects for someone who does not have adequate social support, suffers from chronic health problems, has no private savings, and who was never been employed in a permanent post. Other considerations that research suggests are important moderating influences on our retirement experience include: satisfaction with work (versus "burnout"); the degree to which work met our profound psychological needs (e.g. for recognition or self-esteem, making it hard to detach from or replace work); our attitude to work (necessary evil or something that is pivotal to finding meaning in life); how family and friends view retirement (is it "the done thing," a sign of success; or is it a sign of weak moral fiber, a suspect "work ethic"?); and other economic considerations (e.g. current economic climate; social security provision; government policies).

Consider the so-called "Whitehall II study," which evaluated the impact of several of these factors: 618 London civil servants aged 54 to 59 who were still working were compared over a three-year period on their self-reported mental health with 392 retired colleagues.[14] Job satisfaction (e.g. how much opportunity there was to utilize skills or make decisions about one's work), physical functioning, and three widely-differing job grades were also considered (salaries ranging from a maximum of £11,000 in the lowest grade to £150,000 in the highest grade, in 1995). The results indicated that mental health deteriorated among those still at work, but improved in the retirees, although these improvements were only achieved by those in the highest-paid jobs. Physical functioning deteriorated for both groups.

This study confirms the importance of contextual factors, and psychological theory would expect them to have a large influence on our stress-coping transactions, affecting the outcomes (although unfortunately the Whitehall II study did not measure coping). Some experts assess these contextual factors as a balance between resources and deficits. In Trevor's case, the significance of work became strikingly evident when he stopped utilizing his entrepreneurial talents, and with it his personal identity changed. In effect, retirement had tipped his personal balance sheet upside down. Similarly, Trevor's experience of marriage was consistent with the research findings, which indicate that a negative relationship can rupture the process of transition to retirement, while losing a partner during the transition is both a high risk event and an even bigger blow. Relationships seem to frequently falter during the transition to retirement, due to the extra stress on the relationship, partly because familiar patterns of mutual power and influence are disrupted, partly because of domestic financial pressures. Some of these couples seek therapy, which seeks to bolster their coping skills through enhancing their communication, problem-solving skills, and intimacy.

## Redundancy and the Need for Work

One stressor that definitely belongs near the top of any list of stressors is unemployment, and it clearly featured in Trevor's retirement experience. What is it about work that makes it so important? Why should redundancy be especially problematic? It is hard to exaggerate the importance of work in many societies. This is because it serves profound human needs for structure, meaning, social status, money, and much more. Perhaps particularly for successful people who have a driven, achievement-focused personality, there is a distinct challenge in finding a way to replace job satisfaction. Very few will find such traditional activities as gardening, golf, or socializing sufficient. They may then seek additional stimulation through taking on consultancy or voluntary work, at least for those who had satisfying careers, as with Trevor. By contrast, those who were glad to finish work may feel more comfortable with low-key retirement activities. It appears that for many workers who may not have the opportunity for consultancy or other short term work, retirement can be particularly challenging. According to the authors of the book *Coping with Aging*, "it is not unreasonable to suggest that the loss of the opportunity to work presents a widespread, if not universal, aging crisis that must be coped with even if we do not need to work for income."[15] This is because there are psychological needs that may have been satisfied within the workplace (such as those for stimulation and self-esteem) that are unmet in retirement. I will return to the importance of work in Chapter 2.

## Retirement, Social Support, and Close Relationships

Another facet of Trevor's retirement experience was his divorce. It appears that for older generations in particular, tradition dictates that the woman takes charge of the household and social life. If the wife is no longer present, the husband has to attempt to manage the demands of daily living, and also perhaps replace social support. Furthermore, whereas perhaps women tend to have female confidants, it may be true to say that men are traditionally stoical and disinclined to talk openly to others about their emotions. This kind of triple experience is seen by some as the explanation for the tendency of men in particular to re-marry in order to try and re-build their domestic, emotional, and social lives.

The altered nature of the relationship may also precipitate divorce. Again focusing on the male side of the equation for now, there is the added complication for men that they can, if they don't find some suitable activity out of the home, interfere with the traditional balance. Although well-meaning, they may interfere with the smooth running of the home, getting under the feet of their partner through boredom and feeling isolated when "the girls" get together for a social lunch, as they have routinely done. This represents difficulties for both parties, as the wives might well wish that their husbands would find suitable distractions of their own, which may be compounded by feelings of mutual guilt.

## Conclusions

This chapter has revolved around the case study of Trevor's retirement, as we have considered the various social and psychological aspects of his experience. Of course he is not alone, and studies confirm that about one-quarter of those who retire experience negative and upsetting events. While writing this chapter I came across the striking illustration of Peter Froggatt, the retired vice-chancellor (i.e. Chief Executive) of Queen's University, Belfast . In a talk to the retired members forum of the British Medical Association, he reported "two shocks . . . being unceremoniously dumped on the sidewalk (having wallowed in domestic luxury of living in one of the grandest mansions in Belfast, at the university's expense)"[16] and the deprivation of all the excellent support he had previously received (such as three personal assistants and five full-time secretaries). He also noted a third shock, this time affecting his wife, arising from suddenly being at home far more of the time, sometimes not going out at all. He experienced psychosomatic symptoms (including indigestion, tinnitus, and headaches): it was "as if my nervous capacity was a finite quantity that I used up in the line of duty, and now there is none left over."[17] This meant that it became difficult to handle stressful situations, and gradually "my sunny disposition deserted me."[18] Thankfully, Peter eventually made sense of his situation, in terms of a vicious cycle that he had slipped into: we will resume his tale in the next chapter. He ended his tale by noting a "recipe for contentment,"[19] based on moderation, a balanced lifestyle, and in re-discovering one's true purpose in life.

In response to the nasty surprises that retirement can bring remember my RECIPE for improving matters:

**R**esources (e.g. sufficient money)
**E**xercise
**C**oping strategies
**I**ntellectual activity
**P**urpose
**E**ngagement (social support)

This RECIPE provides an upbeat, constructive perspective where I take the view that human development can be fostered through coping adaptively with the stressors faced in retirement, making retirement an energizing and fulfilling period. In the chapters that follow I set out just how this RECIPE can be followed, starting with the crucial aspect of effective coping strategies.

# 2

# Understanding Retirement

What does it mean to grow old successfully? Some liken it to a ripening process, a natural progression towards a contented state of mind. This might arise from a sense of satisfaction with the stages of life that you have worked through in order to get this far. This is consistent with Shakespeare's seven ages of man in *As You Like It*, which implies a stage on which we play our part, indicating an unfolding of events that are beyond our control. Shakespeare's account is rich in the grudging acceptance of the different parts: "the whining school-boy ... the [lover's] woeful ballad ... last scene of all ... this strange eventful history ... mere oblivion, sans teeth, sans eyes, sans taste, sans everything."[1]

Recent expert opinion and research on human development has suggested an alternative perspective on successful aging. This is based on the idea that, far from some passive process of maturation, our development is driven by our active, persistent, and adaptive efforts to deal with the various stressors in life: "It is not stress that kills us. It is the effective adaptation to stress that allows us to live."[2] To be fair to The Bard, he also recognized stress as a stimulus for development: "sweet are the uses of adversity, which, like the toad, ugly and venomous, wears yet a precious jewel in his head."[3]

Erikson, a psychoanalyst trained in Vienna, is well-known for suggesting that we need to work our way through nine stages of development to reach a successful, mature old age. According to Erikson, each stage was attained by overcoming challenges throughout our lives, causing us to repeatedly exercise our ability to manage stressors. He said: "When no challenges are offered, a sense of stagnation may well take over";[4] and "I am persuaded that only by doing and making do we become."[5] For example, in our youth,

*The Psychology of Retirement: Coping with the Transition from Work*, First Edition. By D. Milne.
© 2013 D. Milne. Published 2013 by John Wiley & Sons, Ltd.

the tasks involve developing a sense of meaning in our life to enable us to build a personal identity, thereby allowing us to develop a full life. On this view, growing old successfully is based on effectively managing the demands of life, in ways that strengthen and fulfill us, as appropriate to the different stages. To illustrate, a challenge in retirement is to adjust to sensory losses with patience and good humor (e.g. deteriorating hearing or vision), while retaining integrity and optimism. According to this logic, to achieve an age of fulfillment based on our resilience, hard-won accomplishments and continuing good health is perhaps the pinnacle of our existence. Now is our time for flourishing and thriving.

As introduced in Chapter 1, the everyday and psychological term for these efforts at managing daily challenges is "coping." This term captures the dynamic, fluid nature of managing life's demands. It is an ongoing process, a kind of juggling act, testing us and strengthening us when we succeed; but demoralizing us if the challenge exceeds our capacity to cope. However, humans regularly demonstrate the ability to transcend even the most extreme stressors, whether in response to health problems (e.g. cancer), incarceration (e.g. Auschwitz), or near-death experiences (e.g. accidents), as revealed through many an autobiography and documentary. Therefore, we need to recognize, as did Shakespeare in his "uses of adversity," what researchers call "stress-related growth" and "transformational coping" (as reflected in old proverbs: "It is an ill wind that blows no good"; "the wind that does not break the tree makes it grow stronger".)

Another common way that things can go wrong with this process is that coping becomes inappropriate or "maladaptive," leading to harmful psychological and/or physical conditions. To illustrate, the notion of a "country of old men" is used to refer to older adults who cope by withdrawing from social interaction and who are focused inwardly, and who are passive rather than active in their attempts to manage stressful life events. Instead of "ripening naturally," people who implement this withdrawn pattern may regress to more primitive attempts at coping, such as avoidance or escape (e.g. through alcohol use or substance misuse). While these can provide short-term respite, such coping strategies are maladaptive, as they are unlikely to result in thriving, wellbeing or personal fulfillment. There are, however, circumstances where such seemingly maladaptive coping makes sense, as when we face unmanageable short-term stressors (e.g. an accident) or chronic long-term difficulties (e.g. caring for someone with a dementia).

This leads us to a third and final view of retirement, one in which the roles of stressors and coping strategies are amplified by the growing constraints and losses that accompany aging. Managing this situation has been viewed as a kind of developmental balance-sheet, involving maximizing the gains while minimizing the losses. This account of retirement emphasizes the heightened need to adjust our expectations and goals, so that we remain organized and purposeful, focused on what is achievable, channeling our time and energy. As we grow older, the balance is thought to continue to shift towards an increasing need to put our available resources into managing physical and mental decline, so as to limit our losses. For example, if we have always jogged and have the aim of continuing this into retirement, then we may need to increase the time we spend training, which means giving up other activities. We may also need to give more attention to our diet or equipment (to manage injuries or pain), which takes up other resources (time, energy, and money) and may adversely affect relationships through becoming selfish or pernickety. These are choices you may wish to make, if jogging is a major goal. This process of selecting goals (S), optimizing areas of growth (O: e.g. taking up sketching and painting), and counteracting losses (C) is thought to characterize resilience.[6] An example from research shows how older adults successfully compensated for their slower hand speed in a typing experiment by reading further ahead (in the text they were copying) than the younger participants, so equalizing the time taken. Another facet of compensating for physical losses is turning increasingly to age-friendly environments and aids (prosthetics, such as hearing aids and loops). A case study example that has been cited in support of this SOC view of retirement is that of the concert pianist Arthur Rubenstein. In a television interview he was asked how, as an 80-year old, he managed to maintain such a high level of skill. He replied that he played fewer pieces (S), practiced more (O), and increasingly slowed the slow passages, so that the faster bits seemed as fast as ever (C). Anticipating this SOC account, Erikson had his own example: "it is natural in the ninth stage to find oneself on the upward course of a steep hill ... so the pack on your back must also be considered ... and the consistent care necessary to keep the body machinery functioning ... in spite of ... deterioration."[7]

The SOC perspective on retirement highlights an often neglected type of resource, the effort and ingenuity we have at our disposal to cope with losses. Whether because of maturation, coping, or the SOC process, research on coping throughout life's stages suggests a surprisingly positive outcome. It appears that rather than stagnating or declining, people usually continue to develop effective and suitably mature coping strategies during their retirement. There is also a sense that coping is more important at this stage in life, as the loss of our physical and mental ability with aging can appear threatening. Through such adaptation, aging can be associated with positive attributes: altruism and humor, cunningly effective coping strategies (wisdom), influence, and a rich sense of belonging. There need be no end to our personal struggle for flourishing and fulfillment.

In order to reflect on this positive, constructive emphasis, a closer look at this vital concept of coping is called for, the "C" in the RECIPE that I offered in Chapter 1. In effect, how can we cope most effectively with the stress of retirement? To determine strong guiding principles, some relevant research and theory will be considered. To illustrate the main aspects of the coping process, we will consider the case study of Donald, a teacher who retired prematurely.

## What is "Coping"?

Chapter 1 provided an outline of coping, together with some related concepts (personality; character; stress; appraisal; distress). A further, in-depth assessment of coping is warranted at this stage as it is central to the aim of this book: the transition to a successful retirement. The word "coping" has a long history and is evident in the vocabulary of the fifteenth century, when it meant "the shock of combat." More recent definitions continue this military tone, including "coming to blows with" and "joining in battle." A current definition, from the Concise Oxford English Dictionary, gives an alternative understanding: "the top, typically sloping or curved, course of a stone wall."[8] These connotations summarize the sense of struggle to manage the demands of everyday living, and, as this captures the situation well, the word "coping" has been adopted by psychologists and others in their therapeutic work.

Freud introduced the notion of psychological coping into public consciousness in the twentieth century. He suggested that people cope by unconsciously defending their wellbeing, as if there were some secret system, like a psychological immune system, protecting us from harm. Freud believed that this protection came through mental "tricks," such as "denial" (i.e. refusing to acknowledge a desire, or a danger, as in a cancer sufferer disbelieving the specialist advice that they are seriously ill). Other common examples of unconscious coping include "intellectualization" (attempting to remove or reduce a threat by treating it in a rather cerebral, theoretical way) and "repression," a defensive strategy that helps us to cope by keeping unacceptable desires out of conscious awareness. A rather surprising example of intellectualization can be found in the edition of Erik Erikson's book that includes the ninth and final stage of the life cycle, where his wife Joan noted their own paradoxical unawareness of "death's door": "Although at age eighty we began to acknowledge our elderly status, I believe we never faced its challenges realistically until we were close to ninety ... we had still taken the years ahead for granted."[9]

In keeping with maladaptive coping, Freud thought that excessive reliance on such unconscious defenses would lead to major problems, such as neuroses (e.g. anxiety or depression). Freud's suggestion that there was an unconscious part of our mind operating in a subtle way was generally unacceptable at the time and caused initial outrage and indignation. Today, most of us perhaps take the view that these unconscious coping mechanisms do exist, but that they are only one form of coping. This is significant, as by definition we require to have conscious awareness of other forms of coping if we are to succeed in making the most of retirement. As this book aims to encourage you to develop conscious coping strategies, little more will be said of Freud's perspective on the role of the unconscious in human development.

In modern psychology, "coping" has been defined as "an ongoing process of personal adjustment that enables individuals to maintain their functioning during stressful periods, but also, a specific, deliberate and effortful process of thinking, feeling and behaving to reduce or remove stress (and the associated emotional or physical distress), leading us to maintain our wellbeing and to develop as a person."[10] This extends the concept of coping beyond its original meaning: unlike a coping stone, it is an ever-changing organic process, an interaction between us and our social world. In contrast to Freud's perspective, coping was best viewed not simply as an unconscious process but also as a deliberate form of social transaction, a give-and-take relationship where, for example, the cut and thrust of debate results in a strengthening of our shared understanding of the topic, or the improvement of our critical powers. Another analogy could be with our immune system: as it fights infection it strengthens the immune response, so empowering the individual and minimizing the effect of the bacteria. In short, through the effort of managing life's stressors, we stand to develop and thereby begin a new phase of development and growth.

As outlined in Table 2.1, researchers consider coping to be a combination of "approach" and "avoidance" strategies, two diametrically different ways of thinking, behaving, and feeling. The approach-based coping strategies are most often associated with good outcomes, so they are usually termed "adaptive" (e.g. analyzing your situation logically and re-appraising it in a more helpful light). Less promising strategies are the avoidance-based

**Table 2.1** The basic coping strategies, with examples from Donald

| Basic coping strategies | Donald's specific coping methods, plus examples |
| --- | --- |
| *The cognitive approach*: addressing a stressor by the way that you think about it | *Logical analysis* – thinking about how to solve a problem, such as resuming teaching on a part-time basis in a new school. |
| | *Positive reappraisal* – reframing or in other ways thinking about things in a positive way, such as recalling how to be an effective teacher in a supportive school. |
| *The behavioral approach*: addressing a stressor by the way that you act | *Seeking guidance and support* – e.g. talking about a problem with a close friend, such as reviewing retirement setbacks with his wife. |
| | *Taking problem-solving action* – e.g. following a considered plan, such as starting the new, part-time post in ways that draw thoughtfully on Donald's main strengths. |
| *Cognitive avoidance*: avoiding thinking about a stressor | *Cognitive avoidance* – e.g. trying to forget about what caused the retirement plan to backfire. |
| | *Resigned acceptance* – thinking that things will never be the same again, as in Donald feeling that his mental acuity was reducing. |
| *Behavioral avoidance*: avoiding dealing with a stressor | *Seeking alternative rewards* – engaging with other activities to avoid the problem, as in singing in the choir. |
| | *Emotional discharge* – "letting off steam" or in other ways venting negative feelings, such as criticizing staff at the old school. |

ones, such as trying to forget about something that happened or "resigned acceptance." Table 2.1 summarizes researchers and clinicians' understanding of the main coping strategies. The case study in this chapter further illustrates the importance of good coping strategies.

## What is "Good" Coping?

The understanding of coping as detailed in Table 2.1 indicates "good" (adaptive) and "bad" (maladaptive) strategies. However, as an ever-changing process, it is difficult to identify a particular way of coping that will always prove successful. For instance, humor is not always helpful or adaptive, but should be judged by its effectiveness within a particular situation. As noted earlier, occasionally a so-called maladaptive strategy, like denial or drinking alcohol, may be adaptive in the short-term (e.g. when the stress becomes unbearable and no other assistance is available). Due to this variable effectiveness, it is best to monitor the consequences of using a particular coping strategy and adjust your methods depending on the results. This is referred to in Chapter 1 as becoming a "personal scientist": we are wise to experiment with different coping methods and observe their effectiveness.

Successful coping is therefore those attempts at managing situations that lead you to feel more personally comfortable and effective, rather than something that is automatically defined by a list of strategies: lists like Table 2.1 have their value, but should be treated with caution. This is in accordance with the aforementioned definition concerning adapting to the demands we face in life, in the same way that Darwin discussed evolution as a struggle for survival by a species. That is, as a result of this coping effort there is a process of adjustment, which may be negative, neutral, or positive. The traditional version of negative coping includes Freud's defense mechanisms, considered to be lower-level coping strategies, concentrating on primitive sections of the brain featuring rigidity, distortion, and automatic response. By contrast, higher level coping responses originate in the newer, outer layer of the brain and tend to be more flexible, deliberate, proactive, and reality-focused. In this sense, the kind of coping that is emphasized in this book is an active and conscious effort to address the demands that we face during retirement. It is more than simple defending or protecting as it involves an effort to develop into the kind of person we wish to become, necessarily assisted by the stressors of our ever-changing world. This may seem paradoxical, but "good" coping moves us beyond simply defending ourselves against a hostile world, allowing us to mature by developing an improved coping repertoire, leading to heightened self-esteem. Therefore, deciding whether or not coping is "good" requires us to study the consequences or effects within the particular context that coping has been implemented. If it results in dealing actively with a stressor through personal adaptation (e.g. by thinking about a problem in a fresh, constructive way), and the intended outcomes are achieved (e.g. more cooperation with a partner), then we judge it to be successful. Examples include:

- *resolving a conflict*: managing to minimize or remove something stressful, such as an argument;
- *reducing physical discomfort*: easing physical distress, such as pain;

- *minimizing psychological distress*: alleviating emotional discomforts, such as anxiety;
- *improving social functioning*: enhancing our relationships, such as joining a club;
- *resuming normal patterns of functioning*: re-engaging with important aspects of our life, such as using a special talent or skill (e.g. playing a musical instrument; sketching; dancing; writing);
- *promoting the wellbeing of others*: coping in ways that benefit family and friends, such as providing emotional or practical support;
- *enhancing positive self-esteem*: coping in ways that allow us to form a favorable view of ourselves, as in developing a sporting talent; and
- *building confidence*: coping in ways that strengthen self-belief, such as testing ourselves in particularly stressful conditions (e.g. competing at sport).

These coping strategies are embedded within a set of related factors, as detailed in Chapter 1. These may be major life events, like moving home, or challenging tasks such as social events or health difficulties (e.g. coping with a disability). Figure 2.1 details these factors as part of the "context" for coping.

## An Example: Coping with Imprisonment

At the time of writing, Ingrid Betancourt, a survivor of a major life stressor, has just published a book detailing her ordeal.[11] She was imprisoned by the revolutionary armed forces group, Farc, in Columbia, in 2002. Having been a Columbian presidential candidate, she was campaigning around the country as leader of the Green Party. Her car was stopped at a roadblock and she was taken prisoner by Farc. Her book, *Even Silence has an End*, tells the amazing story of her ordeal. During her six years in captivity she was beaten, starved, forced on long marches through virgin rain forest, and constantly threatened with a bullet in the head. In the Farc camp she and another prisoner were kept in a hut measuring six feet by four feet with a hole in ground swarming with flies for a toilet. They only had one book between them and nothing else was provided to help them to remain functional. Their only pastime was to annoy each other. There was also the threat of sexual violence from the guards, and Betancourt includes a note on the exploitation of the female prisoners within her book (in addition to

**Figure 2.1**  Coping is like juggling, trying to keep stressors like relationships or finances in hand

the casual obscenities to which they were subjected). In addition, she found the jungle a terrifying environment, particularly the absence of any sign of civilization. In many ways she perceived this lack of any links to her old identity as the biggest stressor. How could anyone possibly survive?

In starting to cope with her situation she realized that she had to re-invent her sense of self: "we lost the compass of what was good and what was right. In captivity, everything is upside down."[12] Re-telling her ordeal to *The Guardian*'s Emma Brockes in October 2010, she began to cry quietly: "you're completely naked. And then you have to face who you are."[13] A crucial part of her survival was that she was captured alongside her assistant, providing vital moral support. Over time, her own sense of proportion became distorted and she began to think that the soldiers had the right to abuse her. She began to understand how she too could become cruel under certain conditions.

It was at around this low point that she made a decision that she would not compromise on certain principles. Among these, she would not answer to a number. Another coping strategy was to attempt to escape, but the first attempt failed as she was too disgusted to drink the muddy water from the jungle puddles, and so returned to the camp. She then put herself into a fitness training program and made herself drink from these puddles, until she knew that she could tolerate the water. She also made a floatation device and set off down river without knowing what lay ahead (starvation or death). When asked about her coping strategies Betancourt said that two things had helped. The first was drawn from something that a guard had said to her when she'd asked if he was frightened by the jungle. He said "we're all going to die. For me, it could be a tree that falls on my head, it could be an anaconda, it could be a bullet from the enemy. I don't care. I'm not going to live my life frightened because of all the dangers around me."[14] She found that very helpful, alongside a second "psychological trick." She realized that rather than mastering her fear she had to accept being scared while focusing on the minutest details of her moment-to-moment existence. She focused hard on specific actions, as in the attention she gave to forcing her hand to grab branches as she went through the jungle. She found that in this way she could: "go beyond the fear. . .put the fear aside and do the basics."[15]

All her escape attempts failed and she was ultimately rescued by Columbian soldiers. Dressed as Farc soldiers and arriving in helicopters, the soldiers told the camp commander that they were moving the prisoners to a different location. Once airborne, the 15 prisoners, including Betancourt, were told that the soldiers were in fact the Columbian national army: "You are free."

Being free however, had its difficulties: her father had died while she was in captivity, her teenage children had grown up, and her marriage was over. Ingrid Betancourt still has to cope with nightmares relating to her captivity (nightmares of being trapped in a building and having to fight her way out), but since being rescued she has set up a foundation to help released hostages, written her book, decided that she would learn to cook for her loved ones, and that she would "always have flowers in my room . . . I understood that in my life I had abandoned too many little pleasures, taking them for granted."[16] Far from the experience of imprisonment destroying her faith in human nature, she believes that it confirmed her belief in her "endless thirst for happiness."[17]

Ingrid Betancourt's coping strategies were implemented in the context of extreme deprivation in rare and unusual circumstances that cannot be compared to everyday life events. However, it can be seen that she successfully developed thinking strategies which allowed her to adapt and survive, both while captive and following her release. These same thought processes exist in all of us, we only need to recognize our potential to cope, whatever life challenges face us.

## Research Findings

In the past 30 years or so, researchers have begun to consider how the way we cope changes as we age. In one US study[18] over 2,000 men and women aged between 18 and 65 years were asked to talk about things they found to be stressful and the efforts they made to cope. It seems from this research that while all age groups engaged in efforts to cope, the older people were less likely to turn to others for advice and more likely to resort to thoughtful reflection. In another study in the 1980s, over 200 men and women aged up to 70 years of age were studied.[19] Those in the 60 to 70 year group were found to use more emotion-based coping and less problem-solving strategies than those in the two preceding decades. Also, the oldest group sought help less often than those in the other age groups. However, an important gender difference was reported, as women sought help more often than men, across all of the sampled ages. In a rather colorful illustration of these age-related differences, one study recruited people of different ages to participate in a miniature golf competition. The results confirmed that middle-aged and older participants coped least well due to the loss of certain performance skills, becoming more physiologically aroused (increased heart rate) and reporting greater anxiety. The researchers attributed these findings to an age-related decline in concentration. However, such negative findings are not without question. In a second experiment that required participants to report the need for repairs to a landlord or manage a lack of promotion at work, adults aged between 20 and 78 years demonstrated differing patterns of coping.[20] The coping strategies were classified into six groups: problem-focused, action-orientated, cognitive problem analysis, passive–dependant behavior, avoidant thinking and denial. Trained researchers rated the effectiveness of the coping responses of the different age groups in each of the two situations. The findings indicated that effective problem-solving skills *increased* steadily with age, the young adults

(20–34 years) were significantly less effective than those in the 55–78 year age group.

These findings indicate that a better developed and more mature judgment is required to clarify the best way of dealing with certain stressful situations. To illustrate, one study that looked at five well-defined everyday conflict situations indicated that the 106 older adults in the study (65–92 years of age) used avoidance-based coping less often than those in middle-aged when handling conflict in authority situations.[21] However, no differences were found between the age groups when dealing with issues such as defeat in competition, general frustration, and disagreement with one's peers. Both groups favored the use of problem-solving in their efforts to manage all types of conflict. In general, research findings suggest that older adults (65 +) are less prone to using escapist coping techniques and more likely to attempt to directly manage conflict or stress. Older people are, in general, less prone to frustration and more willing to meet life's challenges in a cheerful manner, whereas younger people tend to use confrontation or denial, distancing themselves from conflict and other stressors. This seems to be part of a process whereby adults tend to become more self-sufficient as they age, engaging in positive re-appraisal and acceptance of responsibility.

However, one should add a note of caution: many of the above findings are based on comparisons of different age groups at a given time (the "survey" approach). Such comparison is fraught with difficulty, as various other factors may obscure the true relationship between age and adaptation. A better way to clarify how age affects coping is to study the same people over time (the "longitudinal" approach). One such study assessed a group of 95 men over a 40-year period, and an increase in the use of adaptive coping strategies (and a parallel decrease in their use of maladaptive strategies) was found in the adolescent group, through to those over 35 years of age.[22] The study also confirmed that this group demonstrated stable coping mechanisms. Examples of adaptive coping include the finding that these older people were less likely to vent feelings, engage in escapist fantasies, or to have hostile reactions (in comparison with their own coping strategies at an earlier age). It should also be recognized that the various studies of the effect of age on coping are far from unanimous in their conclusions. Some studies find that coping continues to improve up to middle age, after which there is little change; while other studies suggest the kind of continuing development of coping described above. Clearly, there is a third category, involving disease processes such as dementia, which will naturally impoverish and diminish coping strategies over time.

What can we learn from this? It appears that those who cope effectively tend to use a wide range of coping strategies, and continue to use and refine those that work best throughout their lifetime. Also, vital judgment tends to be exercised in terms of the relationship between particular coping strategies and the particular circumstances. Effective "copers" recognize that there is not a fixed relationship between a particular method of coping and a successful outcome, as much depends on the nature of the stressor or demand. It is also important to recognize that life events may jeopardize well-established coping responses. Life crises such as divorce, retirement, accidents, illness, and financial difficulties may diminish our capacity to cope, at least in the short-term. Most people find, however, that as they live with these crises, ways are found to cope and come to terms with the effects.

## The Example of Loneliness

A common aspect of growing old is becoming lonely and research casts light on the reasons for this. For one thing, friends and contemporaries often become less able to interact with us (perhaps due to mobility or hearing problems); and then there is the sad business of bereavements affecting our friends and family, reducing our social network and increasing our isolation. A third reason for loneliness arises from the way that we view such changes to our circumstances. Loneliness is a state in which the individual appraises their circumstances as lacking human intimacy. This can impact through emotional isolation (i.e. a lack of human attachment, preventing the experience of social bonding), and is perceived as a negative or unpleasant situation. This may include the absence or inadequacy of friendships, family contacts, or different kinds of social or community relationships (i.e. we can feel lonely even when we have a strong social network). Whatever the cause, loneliness is associated with mental health problems and psychological pain: numerous studies have documented the link between loneliness and depression, especially for older women. Other research indicates associations with elevated blood pressure, alcohol abuse, dietary problems, obesity, smoking, personality disturbances, faster aging, physiological decline, and suicide. This makes it vital that we employ adaptive, effective coping strategies to prevent or relieve our loneliness. These may involve attempts to find solutions through rejoining society by calling old friends, joining social clubs or special interest groups, pen pal programs, telephone support groups, undertaking voluntary work, or visiting family members. Maladaptive coping strategies, such as wishful thinking and fantasy engagement, may help such problem-solving, as they may enable decisive action to be taken, thereby allowing us to improve our social interaction. Such strategies may also allow creativity in determining how loneliness might be minimized. However, if such wishful thinking were the only coping strategy, it is likely to prove less effective than if taking positive action. Indeed, research suggests that lonely individuals who make successful adjustments employ a variety of coping strategies. One study identified four outcomes: "active solitude" (the creative use of time spent alone), "spending money" (a distracting reaction), "social contact" (an attempt to address isolation by reaching out to others), and "sad passivity" (a form of lethargic self-pity). The way that we view our situation has the power to alter its impact, therefore, "active solitude" recognizes that being alone is not always unpleasant, because for some of us (at least for some of the time) it may represent a welcome haven from difficult social relationships or an opportunity to do something productive or enjoyable.

Another option to reduce loneliness is by increasing involvement in pastimes or hobbies. In an Australian study in 2007 a diverse group of 19 retired people over 65 years old were interviewed about their loneliness.[23] These people were living independently but had differing economic, marital, and health statuses. Almost all of them regarded themselves as being lonely at least some of the time, which was perceived as a natural part of growing old, but a few considered themselves chronically lonely. All felt it was important to be proactive in making contact with others, often around meals (especially on special occasions, like Christmas or birthdays), and social drinks (a cup of coffee or a glass of wine represented good ways to engineer a social meeting). Underpinning these activities was a wish to feel valued and useful to their extended family in particular (e.g. looking after grandchildren and family pets). Indeed, having their own pets was seen as a definite source of companionship, as well as an encouragement to take exercise. They also rated solitary activities as having the capacity to ease loneliness, such as shopping trips, gardening, watching television, and reading (an important "window on the world"). Solitary activities such as gardening have value as they are instrumental in meeting certain psychological needs. By providing a sense of purpose and usefulness, they can be stimulating, tangible, and contribute to a sense of satisfaction, accomplishment, and self-worth.

A second study attempted to understand which factors contributed to loneliness by interviewing 200 people in Chicago, aged between 50 and 68 years.[24] Questionnaires that assessed loneliness were also completed. The questionnaire used, "The University of California Loneliness Scale," has 20 questions concerning general loneliness and feelings of social isolation. Questions include: "I lack companionship" and "there are people I can talk to." Following the assessments, the authors (Louise Hawkley and her colleagues from Chicago University) concluded that people who were unable to engage in social activities (e.g. because of small social networks), and when suffering from poor-quality relationships (in marriage or in wider social networks) were likely to be the most lonely. These findings are unsurprising, but Hawkley and her colleagues also considered personal factors thought to be positively linked to social support (i.e. education, income, and health) and some of the negatively associated factors (e.g. chronic stress). These factors made a significant contribution to explaining the quantity, quality, and loneliness of the relationships of those studied. By contrast, race/ethnicity generally had little influence on loneliness, although the results confirmed higher levels of loneliness in Hispanic and black people. This was attributed to differences in education and income. Improved health and being married also seemed to provide some protection against loneliness. It is worth noting that the marital link was only evident if the marital partner was supportive, defined in terms of being a confidant (i.e. there was intimacy and good communication, even if satisfaction with the marriage was low). The more committed partners in this sample also reported a greater willingness to make sacrifices for the good of the relationship, enhancing their trust in each other, while reducing problematic reactions to marital stressors (e.g. disagreements about money). In this way, stressors appeared to become the basis for greater reliance on one another and deeper commitment, protecting such couples against loneliness (another confirmation that stress is not the cause of distress). Returning to the aforementioned "complaining and verbose" older folk, an interesting aspect of this study was that those with very limited social networks felt less lonely even if they interacted with people deemed "demanding and burdensome" indicating that even "antisocial" support may be better than no support at all! In effect, we can take things like social support for granted, only recognizing its significance when it is absent. Something similar happened to Donald, in the case study, when he stopped teaching.

## Case Study: Donald, a Teacher who Retired then was "Blinded by the Glare of Nothing"

The idea of retirement as a coping process with a strong social dimension is illustrated by Donald's experiences of retirement. Donald began his adult life as a professional musician, working successfully alongside a local musician who eventually made the "big time." As he became "married and mortgaged" he developed a career as an entertainer, but also trained and practiced as a teacher. After some initial uncertainty, Donald found teaching to be a highly satisfying career, becoming Director of Performing Arts and Assistant Head teacher at a secondary school in the North East of England. His was a successful and challenging career, complete with a Masters in Education. However, his role entailed considerable stress, not least in working effectively with those colleagues that he managed. There was also tension concerning the role of the Performing Arts faculty within the school, as the headteacher was a chemist by training and did not fully appreciate the performing arts. Donald was also having physical problems and ultimately required knee replacement surgery. Figure 2.1 illustrates these points in the form of the coping model. This diagram records Donald's social environment (colleagues opposing a greater status for Donald's performing arts department) and some personal factors affected his functioning (knee surgery). Figure 2.1 also illustrates other core elements within the coping model, building on the coping strategies outlined in Table 2.1. In essence, this diagram allows us to understand Donald's retirement predicament, making sense of some key events in his life at that time. This can help us to form a more balanced perspective, and aid decision-making. These environmental factors include many events that are beyond the control of an individual, such as a changing public sector in which schools are expected to transform into "specialist schools," and in which external inspections by the much-feared OFSTED inspectors meant that the goalposts were seen to be shifting (OFSTED is a British government body that inspects schools intended to raise teaching standards).

Indeed, one of the most stressful aspects of this changing environment for Donald was that he began to take on a role in which he became "OFSTED when OFSTED was not here" something that became a tough job, not least because it created a "schism between what I was asked to do and me as a person … I became a lonely voice." A related school factor was the falling numbers of pupils, exacerbating pressure on the teaching staff.

The musical environment had also changed, in that live music had been overtaken by the emergence of the disco. The opportunities that Donald had enjoyed in his early adulthood had virtually disappeared. At the age of 55 years and at the height of his professional ability, Donald decided that he couldn't resist a sudden and unexpected opportunity to retire early: an excellent financial package was offered and he accepted. Knee surgery and his thirtieth wedding anniversary added to the life events he had to cope with at that time. These events represented a transition from someone at the height of his professional career, to someone who had retired. There followed a "year of processing" and attempting to accept that his days could be filled meaningfully by all sorts of DIY jobs, his cooking hobby, and the long-awaited efforts at fulfilling the "pipedreams of youth." However, the fifty-sixth year of Donald's life was far more difficult than expected, and he found it hard to "get myself together." To make matters worse, this was also confusing, because retirement was supposed to be the great opportunity. Instead, Donald felt that his childhood dreams about fantastic musical opportunities were invalid: he found that his half-completed compositions were not coming together successfully and represented a mere "pastiche." He began to feel that he'd let himself down and would not become a successful composer. Areas of opportunity that he had assumed were available, such as composing scores for films, had actually become markets that were difficult to break into. While he'd followed with interest the stories of those who composed music for computer games early and made their millions, he now realized that the world had changed and these opportunities were gone. The emotional impact of these realizations was uncomfortable, as might be expected. At one point Donald felt he could readily have become depressed, feeling that he was a failed pop musician but also disappointed with retirement. The unexpected difficulty of "getting myself together" added to his sense of distress. This was in a context where his wife had cautioned him against immediate retirement, having read about successful retirement being a gradual process of partial retirement. There was also the realization that their marital relationship had been based on extensive and stimulating commonalities: they had both been successful professionals, ascending their respective career ladders in tandem; and they had both enjoyed performing music and in general had enriched each other's lives by their complementary careers. Not least, there was the economic fact that everything had been done in their relationship on a "50:50 basis." The result of this coping situation was that Donald was on the verge of depression and felt "blinded by the glare of nothing." This combination of feeling down and unable to mobilize his resources to get up, left Donald and his wife in a difficult situation.

## Donald's Comeback

Given her discomfort with Donald's retired status and his difficulty in adapting to this major transition in his life, his wife was monitoring the job vacancies and a promising opportunity arose at the local secondary school. By this time Donald had moved into a second home in a rural English county, and such jobs were rare. A further consideration was that the post appeared to offer the opportunity to return to teaching as a teacher rather than a manager. The teaching environment and personal factors were also more favorable. This time the transition was back to teaching, but on a more acceptable and part-time basis. In place of the disappointment and deflation, Donald now regained some autonomy and "enjoyed resuming what I was good at." The cynicism began to evaporate, as teaching was once again fun. It was also something of profound value. Like many older adults, Donald realized afresh how important it was to contribute to the development of others ("generativity," an important phase in later life development). In his case he realized how much he could affect the development of the young teenagers in his classes, and he recognized the power of these relationships in that these youngsters "appreciate what you do." Donald now had a "real role, and a real purpose ... if I don't turn up, 120 kids will miss out." This generativity element helped Donald to enjoy resuming teaching far more than he expected. The social support aspect also improved, with his wife in particular providing significant support for Donald's efforts. Their relationship benefitted too, because now Donald realized that even part-time work "gives the week shape" and provided an endless supply of material to enrich their time together, making it once more balanced, both having interesting lives apart.

## Making Sense of Donald's Retirement Disappointment

Within the literature on retirement there are a number of reasons that are proposed for unsuccessful retirement, and all of these applied to some extent in Donald's case. The first is that the "honeymoon" of retirement is over with the realization of a psychological need for work. That is, after some initial release and euphoria, personal values may arise (e.g. feeling that one has become lazy or useless). The second popular experience is that of re-assessment: following the initial honeymoon, the retired person has space to patiently review and better recognize what retirement means, and to begin to realize what has been lost, particularly the general need for some kind of productive activity that is socially endorsed. A third reason is simply that of boredom, of needing to engage again with meaningful and stimulating challenges. Finally, it has been suggested that lowered self-esteem can prompt a return to work, as we need to exercise our skills or talents to gain approval, recognition, and status (more on this shortly). When I presented these reasons to Donald, he felt that the most relevant was undertaking a re-assessment: "that's me." Regarding the boredom and self-esteem factors, he went on to describe in glowing terms how he thrived on helping a new assistant teacher to develop her career ("gets me out of bed . . . using pathways in my brain again"). He recognized the "kickback" he got by helping this colleague to develop, because she believed in what he did and valued his expertise. This has had a "huge effect on my self-worth, even though it doesn't pay well." All-in-all this has been a surprising and salutary experience for Donald, as he had to recognize that he underestimated the challenge faced in making the transition to retirement. Indeed, he not only "missed teaching like a leg" but confirmed his wife's wisdom: now "she doesn't want to retire"!

## Under-Estimating the Importance of Work

As illustrated by Donald's experience, work can have profound and wide-ranging influences, at least in Western societies, which is why many people find it difficult to adapt to retirement. It is hard to grasp fully just how important work is in defining our lives. As Samuel Johnson put it: "the safe and general antidote against sorrow is employment."[25] Indeed, for many of us there will probably be some significant unconscious denial or only a superficial awareness of the importance of employment, resulting in few of us fully appreciating what the transition from work to retirement will entail.

The case study of Donald illustrates how the transition to retirement can represent a significant loss. In what I regard as a fascinating, highly readable elaboration of the importance of work, the philosopher Alain De Botton has written *The Pleasures and Sorrows of Work*.[26] Here I use his words, linked to my own classification.

a.  *Work meets the psychological need for meaning*: "When does a job feel meaningful? Whenever it allows us to generate delight or reduce suffering in others. Although we are often taught to think of ourselves as inherently selfish, the longing to act meaningfully in our work seems just as stubborn a part of our make-up as our appetite for status or money."[27]

b.  *Work affords the basis for our identity*: "All societies have had work at their centre . . . our choice of occupation is held to define our identity to the extent that the most insistent question we ask of new acquaintances is not where they come from or who their parents were but what they do."[28]

c.  *Work offers a source of happiness*: "For the Greek philosopher, financial need placed one on a par with slaves and animals . . . It was not until the Renaissance that new notes began to be heard . . . references to the glories of practical activity . . . the nobility of labour . . . it now seemed as impossible that one could be happy and unproductive as it had once seemed unlikely that one could work and be human."[29]

d.  *Work as creation*: "How different everything is for the craftsman who transforms a part of the world with his own hands, who can see his work as emanating from his being and can step back at the end of the day or lifetime and point to an object . . . and see it as a stable repository of his skills and an accurate record of his years. . . . (the artist) knows that he is creating something which exceeds him."[30]

e.  *Work as denial*: "How satisfying it is to be held in check by the assumptions of colleagues, instead of being forced to contemplate . . . all that one might have been and now will never be . . . it is a practical stage for clear-eyed action"[31] and "death is hard to keep in mind when there is work to be done."[32]

f.  *Work even feeds the soul*: "the Protestant worldview, as it developed over the sixteenth century, attempted to redeem the value of everyday tasks, proposing that many apparently unimportant activities could in fact enable those who undertook them to convey the qualities of their souls. In this schema, humility, wisdom, respect and kindness could be practised in a shop no less sincerely than in a monastery."[33]

How well do De Botton's claims for the benefits of work stand up to research scrutiny? A test can be found in an issue of the scientific journal, *American Psychologist*, which summarized the benefits of work in 2008.[34] It was noted there that work promotes wellbeing and affords a means for us to gain satisfaction and a sense of accomplishment, linking us to vital social and economic spheres. Work was also regarded as meeting our human needs for survival by providing money with which to live, access to individual social support, a connection to one's culture and to the local social and economic world, and for self-determination (being in control of one's life).

It is claimed that work promotes these benefits by being the main focal point or "playing field" in our lives, encompassing its opportunities, frustrations, challenges, and disappointments. Conversely, redundancy is associated with various mental health problems (anxiety, depression, and substance abuse) as well as relationship difficulties. This adheres to the Victorian idea of work as healing, indicated by the creation of "occupational therapy." Moreover, the loss of work in a community (e.g. due to the closure of a major local firm) has been associated with declining neighborhood quality, including higher rates of crime, violence, and apathy. German research suggests that such problems may never fully resolve for individuals, even when employment resumes, due to damaged self-esteem. In summary, although there are differences with De Botton's claims, research strongly supports the value of work, and this psychology journal concluded that work was "essential for psychological health."[35]

For those in retirement, there is evidence of further benefits. Health psychologists at the University of Maryland found that engaging in part-time work following retirement was associated with improved physical health (in terms of lower blood pressure, less cancer, or strokes), relative to those who stopped work altogether,[36] and those who continued to work part-time in their former careers reported better mental health than those who retired fully.

In view of the profound benefits of work, it is hardly surprising that people like Donald should experience the loss of work as troublesome. Despite knowing the reasons why we work, we may still struggle to recognize the degree to which we actually need work, psychologically speaking. Although in his intriguing way De Botton was referring to paid work, it is surely the case that at least some aspects of these important functions could be served by voluntary or other work. Therefore, in summary, we might well note that retirement signifies the end of paid work, but not necessarily an end to the "sorrows and pleasures of work."

## Vicious and Virtuous Coping Cycles

Another way to make sense of Donald's experience is to think of coping as an ongoing process, one that involves a range of stressors and the successive application of various coping strategies over time. In combination with factors such as social support, coping tends to have a "snowballing" effect, for better or worse. A good example is personality, in that the way we are will affect many parts of our experience. An illustration is that powerful trait of "conscientiousness": within the Longevity Project, which followed 1,500 people for 80 years,[37] it was found that the risk factors and protective "shields" affecting longevity were not random or isolated but bunched together in patterns. Specifically, those who were not conscientious as young boys were far more likely to grow up to have poor marriages, to smoke and drink more, to do less well in education, to fare less well at work, and to die younger. Similar patterns occur with coping. When things are going well, we talk of a "virtuous cycle," as one success follows another, strengthening our confidence and with it our effectiveness: we can do no wrong, feeling confident and effective. For instance, if we have joined a club for social contact and found someone to talk to, this may encourage a quick return and greater involvement, building to true membership of that group, so that it becomes part of one's new identity. When things go less well we can enter a downward spiral, the so-called "vicious cycle," where one setback follows another, weakening our confidence and fostering avoidance, self-pity, blaming others, and so on.

These processes are illustrated in Donald's experience. When Donald first retired he was surprised to discover that life was not that easy, and as things began to go wrong in his life, he struggled to cope effectively, leading him into a vicious cycle that resulted in the onset of depression. He describes feeling "nearly burnt out." However, once he resumed teaching he reversed this cycle, regaining his self-belief and identity. His environment became more congenial and his personal health problems receded. I have illustrated these cycles in Figure 2.2, with examples from Donald's experience. Note that the two cycles are joined by what I call the "coping crossroads," to capture the view that life is an endless series of attempts to cope effectively, and that how we cope will influence which cycle we enter.

This account of coping applies both to a particular incident and to the way we develop throughout our lives, in that dealing with a succession of incidents provides the basis for us to develop into the kind of person we have become, and our tendency to react over time to situations in a particular way. To illustrate these processes, consider again the retirement experience of the leader of Queen's University, Peter Froggatt, first presented in Chapter 1. His wife outlined a couple of his vicious cycles:

> Look, you've got yourself into a lose-lose situation. You either work harder to
> take your mind off the symptoms, which only winds you up more and makes

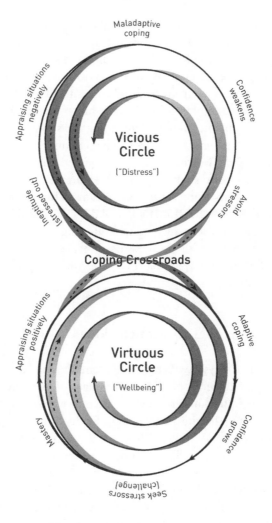

**Figure 2.2** Virtuous and vicious cycles, illustrated with material from David's experience of retirement

the symptoms worse, or you ease up like the doctors tell you to do and that gives you a guilty conscience, which also makes the symptoms worse. You think that you should be able to go on working as you did and also that you must go on working as you did.[38]

No wonder he had been suffering! Thankfully, his wife's understanding of this dilemma served as an impetus to Peter to use fresh coping methods, involving resuming his old hobbies, taking fresh stock of his life's purpose, and regaining a better lifestyle balance. With these adjustments, he progressed across the "coping crossroads" and entered a virtuous cycle where "*everything* clicked into place."[39] This is a rather high-powered example of adapting to retirement, given his demanding and specialized role in running a university, but extreme examples can help to underscore what we understand about coping, which was why I considered the hostage experience of Ingrid Bettancourt. In short, coping with retirement needs to be seen as a complex matter, involving several significant factors which act in concert and can develop a momentum, making it difficult to achieve desired health and social outcomes. The analogy with juggling is a good one, in that we must continue to deal with our stressors as best we can. Therefore, the chapters that follow outline ways that may help you to juggle more effectively with retirement.

## Conclusions

There are myriad ways in which people attempt to cope with the stressors of retirement, and Table 2.1 provides a summary of the main options. These emphasize the importance of how we attempt to respond to the stressors in our life, linking the vital concept of individual coping to our adaptation as a species. As Darwin put it: "It is not the strongest of the species that survives, not the most intelligent, but the one most responsive to change."[40] Research suggests that being responsive includes appropriate goal-setting, open-mindedness, a willingness to experiment (including acting creatively), self-awareness, and optimizing areas of growth while counteracting areas of loss or decline are features of effective responses. In general, some actions are highly promising (e.g. resuming part-time work), but there are also major individual differences in terms of what will foster successful coping. Work itself may not suit all retirees, perhaps especially those who were relieved to conclude an arduous or aversive career.

For those who were fulfilled in their work, there is the possibility that they judge their self-worth by their work that may result in retirement diminishing their self-worth, leaving them feeling empty, deflated, or worse. At such times we need our coping repertoire to remind us what really matters and to allow us to access other sources of self-esteem. Success at work is but one (albeit major) avenue to happiness. Our work should not equate to our worth, so the loss of work should not generate unhappiness. Indeed, the very idea of measuring work (or retirement) in terms of "worth" is suspect, the self-defeating pursuit of an abstraction (like trying to find your "true" self). Questioning about your personal worth since you retired cannot be answered, because we have no agreed metric for our worth. Better to assume that we all have the same intrinsic, unchanging worth, to nurture that, and move on. What promises better results is to set achievable goals, like thinking about how you can heighten the pleasure you get from what you are doing today; to consider how you can communicate caring to the people you talk to; or to puzzle over how you can get closer to mastering a new skill. There is really only one way in which you can lose your feeling of self-worth, which is to take it away from yourself, by being illogical, unreasonable or critical of yourself, or by uncritically accepting how other people respond to you. Therefore, the fundamental conclusion to this account of coping and retirement is that we need to try different approaches to coping if we are to adapt successfully to what life throws at us, and if we are to work progressively towards what we want to become, following the guiding ideas within the book's RECIPE:

**R**esources (e.g. sufficient money)
**E**xercise
*Coping strategies*
**I**ntellectual activity
**P**urpose
**E**ngagement (social support)

The following chapters deal with other concepts of adapting to and enjoying retirement, though coping is the major focus.

# 3

# Reframing Retirement

Active coping is central to retiring successfully, but it does not operate in isolation, being embedded within ways of thinking and feeling that significantly shape our ability to adapt. In the first chapter I noted how stressors trigger appraisals: these are ways of perceiving events, influencing whether we view the stressor as threatening or welcome, manageable, or overwhelming. As these initial appraisals lead to judgments about how to cope with the situation, they influence what follows. Like our general coping efforts, perceptions are not fixed ways of responding, but can develop into a key part of our approach to stress. For example, in sport psychology there is an emphasis on being "positively preoccupied," of reframing everything that happens in as positive a way as possible. An example would be a cricketer, who when asked how he felt about playing on the bone-dry pitches of India might reply: "My favorite surface: nowhere better to play spin bowling." A few weeks later he was in England, being asked about the perfect conditions there for seam-bowling: "My favourite surface: I just love the way that the weather affects the game." At this point he was challenged: "But you said Indian conditions were your favourite!" His reply was that he made himself love wherever he had to play. This person is coping by taking as positive an attitude as possible to unavoidable stress, an approach that is likely to be helpful. As Art Linkletter put it: "Things turn out best for the people who make the best out of the way things turn out."[1]

To regard your unavoidable circumstances or something that happens as an opportunity or a challenge is an example of how we think, as is judging that you have the resources to rise to the challenge. Assuming that such appraisals are sound, this paves the way for adaptive coping and a

*The Psychology of Retirement: Coping with the Transition from Work*, First Edition. By D. Milne.
© 2013 D. Milne. Published 2013 by John Wiley & Sons, Ltd.

resultant sense of confidence and general wellbeing. It is unlikely to help a cricketer to emphasize the difficulties inherent in particular wickets. At the time of writing, I came across this in The Northumbrian magazine: "Even after being abroad, I saw all that can be found in Northumberland. Lots of people in our region don't realize what we have here, be we have it all,"[2] which reminds me of the autobiography of Albert Facey.[3] Albert was a boy whose father deserted him for the gold fields of Western Australia, dying before Albert was age two; whose mother deserted him soon afterwards; who started working in the rough Western Australian frontier at the age of eight, teaching himself to read and write; who fought at the Gallipoli landings; lost his farm in the Depression; lost his son in World War II, then his wife, but went on to call his autobiography *A Fortunate Life*! The book is rich with examples of how to appraise situations positively, anchored in an optimistic philosophy: "I never ever worried about trying something different or having a go at something. I always believed that if you want to do something you usually can."[4] He managed to pack an incredible amount into his 88 years, ending the book with this appraisal: "I have lived a very good life, it has been rich and full. I have been very fortunate and I am thrilled by it when I look back."[5] This is Facey's perception, his personal view of events, rather than some kind of objective truth. There was nothing fixed or inevitable about his upbeat account, and indeed most books of this kind are decidedly less positive, even when the situations encountered are similar. So, how is it that one person can see the world "through rose-tinted glasses," while another has a glass perpetually "half-empty"?

Retirement can be in need of this kind of reframing, especially if the circumstances are difficult. Researchers have studied the impact on retirement: whether it was voluntary or mandatory, how favourably the individual viewed retirement, how the decision was made (especially whether or not they had any control), and whether there a suitable role was available in retirement. Yet as one review stated, "despite the wide range of studies dealing with numerous features of the retirement process, we still know very little about the complexity of the retirement transition as it is experienced by individuals."[6] To understand their experience better, the authors of one US study interviewed 72 professional males and females, aged between 50 and 60. The group included professors, doctors, business personnel, social service professionals, and lawyers. This group had already begun to think about retirement, holding perceptions ranging from an entirely positive view (22 of this sample) through ambivalence (14) to the view that it represented "social death" (from the remaining 50 percent, who were heavily involved in their work, some of whom were very senior employees). Prior research suggests that such "white collar" workers hold generally more positive views of their work and hence somewhat more negative views of retirement. In this sample, the interviewees were most influenced in their perceptions by four factors: whether or not they had unfinished business at work, job satisfaction, financial situation, and health (wealth and health were the most salient factors). Therefore, it would seem that part of the "complexity" of the retirement decision is the way that individuals frame it, which may be colored significantly by these four factors.

A second study was conducted in London, with a sample of 32 people aged between 70 and 80 who were more representative of the general population.[7] Half of this group were thriving, and half were struggling to cope (as indicated by their self-reported quality of life). For them retirement was also perceived in a range of ways, but was generally vividly recalled and took place when they were aged between 60 and 65. Negative perceptions of retirement were associated with sudden exits from work (e.g. redundancy), coupled with thoughts about significant loss, and having the routines provided by work disrupted. For the poor copers, this was linked with excessive drinking, depression, and boredom, as this quote illustrates: "I felt it was a great loss [leaving work] in my life. Not being able to get up in the morning to a regular routine and so on. But talking about my routine it was because of the long hours that I used to do, it was a great loss to me. In fact I felt quite depressed. I was really miserable for the first 18 months, and I'd thought actually I'd quite enjoy it, but I couldn't adjust somehow to the gap that the work left."[8]

The better copers tended to find alternatives to work, having reframed any adversity in the light of successful past experiences, of being able to manage adverse events (e.g. using the extra time to recover from illness). Using the term "resilience" in place of coping, these researchers concluded: "Our data indicate that the process of constructing and reinterpreting past events in the light of more recent ones was essential to developing resilience. This is because it not only allowed people to retain a sense of identity but also seemed to clarify the meaning of adverse experiences. This process appears to create a genuine acceptance and distance between the emotional weight of adversity and day-to-day life. Furthermore ... this process also seemed to help people readjust their expectations to changing circumstances."

These research examples indicate that how we think about our predicament significantly shapes our coping and adjustment. Such thinking naturally draws on the basic assumptions we hold about life, including what we believe to be the reason for working, or how important it is to retire. This is the sphere of our "assumptive world." Psychological theory suggests that we humans share three fundamental, unconscious assumptions. These provide the bedrock or foundation for the way we make sense of our world, being the deeply-held beliefs that provide us with a sense of security, reality, meaning, and purpose. These beliefs develop early on, helping to organize our subsequent experiences, provide a basis for our expectations, appraisals, attributions, and other mental processes. These core beliefs are: that people are basically benevolent; that the world is a meaningful, orderly place (predictable; lawful); and that we are safe and secure (a worthy, decent person). These core assumptions will color the sense we make of the events that overtake us, even though we might say rationally that they are flawed. We will therefore tend to expect others to react positively to our retirement; expect our pension to appear like clockwork in our bank account; and expect to live forever (a core assumption is that we are indestructible, illustrated by the common reaction to tragedy that "I didn't think it'd happen to me"). To illustrate, here are some of the statements from a questionnaire designed to measure these assumptions. The respondent indicates how much they agree or disagree with the statements:[9]

- "Most people can be trusted"; "I believe people are good" (benevolent world).
- "You generally know what will happen tomorrow"; "I feel in control of what happens to me" (world meaningful).
- "Terrible things won't happen to me"; "People are safer than they think" (safe and secure).

We can see the importance of these fundamental assumptions in situations where they have been turned upside down and made conscious, as when we witness acts of terrorism, like the Twin Towers; or have a life-threatening experience. It appears that much of the accompanying distress arises because our assumptions are challenged: the world is not such a friendly place after all, random events can overtake us regardless of how "good" we are. Life-threatening experiences can be overwhelming, causing us to dwell on traumatic incidents (including deliberately re-living events and unconscious "flashbacks"), or to feel confused, insecure, emotionally numb, and unsure of our identity. At its worst, we might experience a post-traumatic stress reaction. As it is the disturbance to our fundamental beliefs that caused the reaction, therapists and others will therefore try to tackle how sufferers think about what happened. The aim is to help the sufferer to assimilate what happened or modify the assumptions, in a way that enables the trauma to fit with their assumptions.

Another example of our thinking, the "constructing and re-interpreting" as identified by the London research (see note 7), is the way that we attribute credit or responsibility for events. In psychology the term "attribution" is often used, and research has included examining how carers behave towards their charges, such as older adults with a dementia living in a care home. The carers' interpretations are understood to pivot on their judgment about whether or not an incident (perhaps wandering, incontinence, or aggression) was due to the individual (did they choose to create the incident?), whether this person had any control, and whether there were any mitigating circumstances. Research suggests that, if the carers regard someone in their care as not personally responsible (perhaps because of an advanced dementia), unable to control what happened (perhaps because of infirmity), and that there was a disruption to the usual care routines (staff were off sick), then they will tend not to attribute responsibility to the person. Based on this way of thinking, the carers are more likely to have sympathy, little or no anger, and a willingness to help the person. Unfortunately, it is often the case that carers' attributions end up assigning responsibility for incidents to the older person ("difficult personality" or similar attribution), leading to little sympathy, more anger, and an unwillingness to help. Such thinking processes (e.g. "they could do more to help themselves") may partly explain other seemingly uncaring situations we read about in our newspapers. This can partly be regarded as "defensive" thinking, in the sense that carers naturally wish to attribute wholesome qualities to themselves, as do we all. Indeed, psychologists' recognize a general tendency for humans to bias their thinking to protect and cultivate their self-image, particularly in the face of conflicting information. We will often do so by re-attributing, rationalizing the situation by claiming to have had no control over the situation, and hence had no choice but to do as we did. This allows us to appraise our actions in ways that are consistent with or even enhance our self-image, minimizing any awkward sense that we may not quite live up to this image (self-protection: called "cognitive dissonance"). In practice, this kind of self-serving bias can help us accept otherwise unacceptable thoughts or behaviors (e.g. when given too much change in error, keeping the money by thinking "well, I need the money more than them"; excusing cheating by downgrading the assessment or belittling the assessor).

Appraisal, assumptions, reframing, and attributions are all involved in how we "perceive" the world. Perception is the highly subjective psychological process of organizing our experience, enabling us to cope. It starts with our senses, which attempt to interpret incoming stimuli to give us a, meaningful understanding of events as they unfold. For instance, if our eyes see something fleetingly, perception creates a coherent picture (there is currently debate about how much of this initial interpretation takes place at the sensory surfaces, as opposed to the sensory centers in the brain). Perception provides us with the most likely explanation for the visual image, based on our personal experience (assumptions), expectations, and motivational state (including the situation we are in). You can almost see this process at work if you gaze at an optical illusion or other ambiguous image, as the brain flicks from one possible explanation of the image to another. For example, Rubin's well known diagram, The Vase, can be seen either as a vase or as two faces.[10] The flicking backwards and forwards between these interpretations every couple of seconds is due to the brain trying to perceive the stimulus correctly, while recognizing that there is a problem in viewing the illusion.

Imagine how this system might backfire if the image or event that we are trying to perceive accurately is affected by expectations and strong feelings, in a challenging environment. Such distorting pressures create a significant perceptual "bias," which may then become increasingly distorted by the subsequent phases of thinking: memorizing, analyzing, decision-making (including how to respond), and evaluation. To illustrate the distortion, we know from a wide range of sources that our ability to see events accurately is rarely consistent with an objective account (e.g. recollections about accidents are at variance with video recordings). This is because, aside from memory distortions or deficient thinking skills, our brains filter what happens to us, applying self-serving biases to help us to cope (e.g. by blaming the other party for an accident or forgetting a personal trauma, to keep intact assumptions about a benevolent world). To relate this directly to retirement, one risk associated with retirement is the loss of social support and subsequent loneliness. However, as noted earlier, this is a risk, not an automatic fate: among other things, the definition of loneliness depends on how it is perceived by the individual – recall that not everyone who is alone is lonely and not everyone who has company feels supported.

As the result of these distortions, our perceptions are often more negative than Facey's, as in viewing a stressor as daunting or overwhelming, leading to an avoidance from something that requires our attention. This applies to minor stressors such as a domestic argument or major events like retirement.

I imagine that if Facey were confronted with the same stressor he would view it as another opportunity to try something different, an opportunity to "have a go." We call this way of thinking "reframing": developing a more adaptive view of our general predicament (i.e. interpreting things in a more positive, balanced, constructive, or realistic way). When we think like this, the "glass is half-full," we "look on the bright side" and "make the most of it," and we free ourselves of self-defeating errors in our thinking. The following case study illustrates reframing, and aspects of perception.

## Case Study: Mae's Positive Perspective

Mae's story clearly illustrates a definite talent when it comes to re-framing her experiences. Up until the age of 56 she had worked as a secretary, taking responsibility for one of the accounts of an airline company. This role represented internal promotion, based on her ability to manage the accounts effectively and her fondness for figures. When the airline was taken over she was offered an attractive redundancy package, which she took because her father was unwell. A small pension from a prior job meant that she could manage financially, so she took the package and focused on keeping her ailing father living in his own home, despite his several health problems and operations. She felt that he "needed nursing and looking after . . . I didn't want him to be alone in the house." There was also a sense of repaying him for being such a good father ("couldn't fault my childhood").

However, five years later, as her father recovered (and is still doing well at the time of the interview, aged 87), Mae decided to resume work. This was because her son had set up his own small cafe, and "he needs me a lot" (e.g. when it comes to making decisions and completing paperwork). She also valued dealing with the customers ("I like meeting people") and trying to help them, many of whom were students. She noted that "they are away from home for the first time, still young and want a bit of comfort." She helps by playing a definite role as a social supporter, listening intently and asking interested questions, in addition to serving them. She views this role as "being a mother, really; don't want them to come to harm." Not surprisingly, this role includes having a chat with them all: "90 percent of them are nice, and with the other ones I try even harder, just to show them!" Being a "mother" includes listening caringly to their woes and worries, which can range from hangovers to concerns about serious illness, and savoring their happy moments. She sometimes takes customers into the office for a chat. One example she gave was of a student with a "thumping headache," to whom she gave some painkillers and a free cup of tea; another was a student who burst into tears, perhaps (Mae guessed) because she was homesick. Embedded in this supportive role is a further reason why Mae is back at work: hearing about other peoples' problems helps her to feel better: "You think you've got problems, but then you see it's not so rosy for others either, so it's not so bad, really."

## Reframing

In this social support role Mae feels a regular need to provide a fresh perspective on her customers' woes and worries. For instance, it might help to view that headache as self-inflicted, a natural consequence of drinking too much the night before. This might end with the advice: "Be more careful." For that homesickness, it may help to adopt the attitude that "it'll be worth it – just try and do it", or "it's not the end of the world."

Her natural tendency to reframe events positively is not limited to her interactions with customers. If the coffee machine breaks down because it's too cold, Mae responds that she's "just got to pack in, as can't make the weather . . . try not to get so frustrated . . . accept it . . . only so much you can do . . . business has its ups and downs."

More generally, her underlying outlook appears to be one of caring and compassion: "Everyone in life has good in them, something to give," enabling her in turn to feel good about helping them. But the most important requirement needed for her own happy life is her family: "If my family are happy, I'm happy." As this illustrates, she sets her sights on modest goals ("don't expect anything") and recognizes that you "have to be happy and content with what you have," though also taking the view that "life's what you make it, every day." She also prizes freedom: "I'm alive and can please myself, to a point."

Mae does acknowledge a degree of discontent in that she feels she should perhaps be more ambitious: "Maybe I should have higher goals." Her son evidently feels ambitious too, as he is studying part-time to gain the qualification needed to resume his first career stating that he "doesn't want to be here." This causes Mae further discontent as this jeopardizes a "viable business . . . reluctant to let it go". Such tensions cast a slight shadow over her happiness, as she occasionally feels that she is making it harder for her son to "stand on his own two feet" feeling she needs to be a bit "harder," or maybe she should gradually withdraw from the business ("Am I trying to live his life for him?"). However, this is balanced by worries about whether the business would suffer: "worries me a bit." I asked if she felt trapped: "Yes, exactly: I want him to be happy. I know in my heart what is right, but just can't say no." A further complication is that Mae has little "me time": "Free time is, very limited" and she'd like to "learn about computers ... go for walks ... get a dog again ... and read, to stimulate my brain." In reading this, you will not be surprised to learn that the dog would have to be a rescue dog ("because it needs a good home")!

Mae's story illustrates how reframing can help us with life in general (through a suitable philosophy or generally positive outlook) and in our everyday interactions with people. It is also clear from her account that reframing is only part of how we need to function if we are to cope successfully: successfully managing life's inherent tensions and worries also requires a sound analysis of the situation, thoughtful decision-making, and the other stages of the thinking process.

## Thinking Straight

Mae clearly analyses situations skillfully, drawing on other aspects of her thinking to arrive at ways of coping effectively. This talent is not to be taken for granted: whether due to biases or other pressures, our thinking can readily go awry in several ways. A sophisticated account of straight thinking is to be found in a renowned book from 1930, called *Straight and Crooked Thinking*, by Robert Thouless. This self-help book was intended to guide "those who wish to learn more of the nature of crooked thinking" to becoming more adept at mastering their thinking and protect themselves against "intellectual exploitation by unscrupulous speakers."[11] For instance, Thouless noted the trick called "the exception proves the rule," where a sound argument is refuted by an extreme instance: "a fairly common trick and ... obviously a dishonest one ... It can be dealt with by pointing out ... that an exception does not prove that a general rule is true, but that it is false."[12] He goes on to note that the word "prove" is used originally to mean "test," which is an honest way to judge whether a rule is true (and which is a cornerstone of modern scientific logic: falsification). Logic is the formal discipline in philosophy for straight thinking, which reduces statements to particular types of argument (e.g. syllogism) and then to symbols, to allow them to be tested systematically. Thouless had a more practical aim. He listed 38 types of faulty ("crooked") thinking, in the form of a self-help manual promoting straight-thinking "remedies." Here are some examples (the italicized terms are the modern versions; the straight thinking remedy suggested for each of these by Thouless is in brackets):

- *Cherry-picking*: Faulty thinking by attempting to prove something by providing a biased example (Straight thinking: "select instances opposing your opponent's contention").[13]
- *Red herring*: A deliberate attempt to divert or confuse a thinking process by introducing misleading material, or by changing the subject ("bring the discussion back to the question ... with care and good temper").[14]
- *Begging the question*: sometimes called *circular reasoning*, this form of crooked thinking argues for a conclusion that has already been assumed in the premise ("Argument in a circle and begging the question are universally recognized as dishonest tricks in argument. In order to refute ... it is therefore only necessary to show that the trick is being used").[15]
- *Black and white thinking*: creating a false dilemma, treating things in an either-or fashion ("Refuse to accept either alternative, but point to the fact that of the continuity which the person using the argument has ignored").[16]
- *Special pleading*: applying additional considerations without proper criticism, as in seeking an exemption without justification; also referred to as *double standards* ("Dealt with by applying one's opponent's special arguments to other propositions which he is unwilling to admit").[17]

Of course, our interest in straight thinking has developed since 1930, perhaps no more so than in the mental health field, with treatments such as "cognitive therapy." Cognitive therapy texts list common examples of "faulty thinking," some of which match those listed by Thouless (e.g. black and white thinking) while others develop a more clinical angle.

- "Catastrophizing": Assuming that the worst possible outcome will ensue.
- "Fortune-telling": Predicting the future, in a negative light.
- "Name-calling": Describing yourself in pejorative terms (e.g. "heartless" or "thick").
- "Wishful thinking": Inhabiting a fantasy world, where magical things just might happen.
- "Personalizing": Inferring a personal significance when none exists (e.g. a constructive suggestion implies personal weakness).

Helpfully, the cognitive therapy field is rich in ideas for tackling such crooked thinking. This includes general ways of thinking straight, and some specific coping strategies that you can apply. To challenge negative thinking, you can ask some basic questions, such as: "What are the facts?"; "Are the words I'm using extreme (e.g. should, must, have to, ought, always, never)?" "How would (someone you respect) view the situation?"; and "What would I think on a day when I was feeling great?" Specific techniques to bolster your coping include maintaining an "alternative diary," where the left-hand column is used to record negative thoughts, and the challenge is to rebut it in the right-hand column, with an alternative perspective. So, "catastrophizing" about your health, because you have a headache ("I knew one day cancer would get me; this feels so bad I must have a brain tumour") would be responded to by writing some straight thinking in the right-hand column (e.g. "what evidence is there that I have cancer? After all, I have had bad headaches off and on all my life, but never had cancer"). A "name-calling" example (one that occurred on the day I write this) was a friend who regarded buying himself a first-class rail ticket as "extravagant" and "self-indulgent," a sign of being morally weak, but who was also able to take an alternative perspective (that it was good for the economy to spend his hard-earned money). Such approaches are well-described in the book *Manage Your Mind*.[18]

Thinking straight is clearly essential to coping successfully with retirement. This can occur on a moment-to-moment basis, in dealing with what cognitive therapists call "automatic thoughts" (e.g. Mae's immediate thought when a customer was rude was "I'll show them"). Effective coping would build on an awareness of these automatic, negative thoughts by rehearsing alternative thoughts. With practice, supported by evidence that the straight thinking was indeed valid (e.g. rude customer becomes polite), we can become more optimistic about events. The goal is to become "positively preoccupied," like an athlete who allows nothing to upset the right focus on the big day, by repeatedly finding alternatives to negative automatic thoughts, and by thinking straight about the interminable difficulties of competition.

Straight thinking also embraces enduring issues and concerns, some of them truly life-threatening, such as how best to cope with a real case of cancer, or how to respond to a dependent relative with challenging behaviors. At the more philosophical end of the spectrum are persistent questions about whether our life is "on track," or whether we should have done more with our life. The way we ponder such issues could have a profound effect on our mood, by bringing us into a virtuous or vicious coping cycle (see Chapter 2). On this point, I believe that straight thinking requires that we consider what the experts think, those philosophers who dwell on what makes for a "good life."

## The Good Life

In the UK, the "good life" is often associated with a 1970s television sitcom (broadcast in the US as "Good Neighbors"). It revolved around a man whose 40th birthday marked a transition, following which he abandoned his job, devoting himself instead to a simple, self-sufficient lifestyle, while continuing to live in his suburban home with his reluctantly like-minded wife. They turn their garden into an allotment, growing as many fruit and vegetables as possible, supplemented by food from their farmyard animals (chickens, pigs, etc.). They even generate their own electricity from the methane emanating from the animal waste. Here then is a couple who have taken an unconventional view of life and how it might best be lived, many years before "green" living became a popular idea. Perhaps they drew strength for this dramatic change in their lifestyle from a profound re-think about their "rat-race" life, coming up with an alternative way to live it.

This issue is also hard to ignore during retirement: how should we live the rest of our lives, and towards what end? The question posed in the philosophy of the "good life" is: what is the most desirable life for a human being? Consideration of the good life aims at identifying the most fulfilling, meaningful, and satisfying life possible for humans, a life which may be described as thriving, flourishing, or blessed (e.g. how might we do something important with our life?). The question of what constitutes the good life has been the subject of philosophy for centuries, identified mostly with Aristotle and Socrates. Of particular relevance to tackling the tricks of perception, the process of formal debate within philosophy hinges on argument, a debate that proceeds from claim to counter-claim, thesis to counter-thesis, so that every point is tested out critically. This process tends to keep our thinking straight, making it a valuable point of reference for our private consideration of the bigger issues, with this reasoning process itself a facet of the good life.

In the Old Testament, the good life is summarized in this statement by the prophet Micah: "He has showed you, o man, what is good; and what does the Lord require of you but to do justice, and to love kindness, and to walk humbly with your God."[19] This may have particular relevance for those with a religious faith. By contrast, the familiar modern-day answer to the question about the most desirable life is perhaps often "to be rich and famous." If you doubt this, browse the popular magazines in your local newsagent. However, such a philosophy is problematic. Reflecting on the experience of the collapse of communism in the Czech Republic, Vaclav Havel (who became President) wrote of the appeal of Western values (i.e. democracy, human rights, the free market) while recognizing their tainted by-products (materialism, "frenzied consumerism" and the "selfish cult of material success").[20] Such tensions question the desirability of a philosophy based on Western values, and can create a crisis of confidence when it comes to deciding on the way we should live. This is especially true in our modern age, where personal autonomy takes on ever greater importance, and where traditional values are questioned. In this era of "liberal individualism," no longer are things like keeping one's promises, honesty, respect, or justice understood according to a time-honored, Biblical, or shared morality. To illustrate, at the time of writing it seems that one of the reasons that the High Street bankers have become such despised figures is that they reject the public's idea of natural justice, the terms of an ethical society. This states that if you are incompetent and cause huge problems for society, then you do not merit a massive bonus and the right to remain aloof from criticism.

Debates on such points go back at least two and a half thousand years, to the Greek philosopher Plato. In one of the dialogues, Plato is represented by Socrates (Plato's teacher). The dialogue is between Socrates and various Greek citizens, as he asks them various questions about what is "good." The citizens tend to argue that what makes something good is that it is successful at getting what you want, regardless of how this affects others. This is thought to be the longest running intellectual disputes in the history of the world, as it still arouses debate. Socrates argued that a good life cannot simply be characterized in terms of getting what you want, since in part its goodness depends on what it is you want, and if you want bad things your life will be bad. That is, there is nothing good or admirable about some actions that get a particular individual what he or she wants. The term in philosophy for this point of view is *egoism*: I should try to get what I want out of life. Clearly there is some crooked thinking behind egoism.

A second philosophical perspective is that of hedonism: the belief that the good life is that which is most pleasurable. On this view, happiness or pleasure is an end in itself, whereas the other goals that we pursue are termed "instrumental," in that we pursue them in order to obtain pleasure later. This is a very similar perspective to egoism, a view in which the good life is as full as it possibly can be of bodily pleasures: food, drink, sex, and so on. However, hedonism does contain one widely-shared view, the idea that the absence of pain is a good thing. Perversely, within the very idea of hedonism is some inevitable pain, due to the excessive indulgence of the body. Another difficulty with hedonism is that this indulgent lifestyle does not appeal to everyone: those who for example value a highly moral or artistic life will find it unworthy; and those who seek wild excitement may find it relatively dull. It also commends only some pleasures, which will inevitably be rather partisan; and distinguishes between "higher" and "lower" pleasures, between pleasure and contentment. There is a famous piece of philosophical reasoning about hedonism: imagine a pig whose life is indeed hedonistic, as compared to Socrates with his strong appreciation of just how little he knows. We can imagine that the pig is satisfied with his life, while Socrates is dissatisfied with his. On this logic, hedonism would appear to commend the life of the pig over that of Socrates. This is so absurd that at this point in the comparison we have to assume that hedonism includes crooked thinking. There is also the awkward business of pleasures that may harm others, such as sadistic pleasures. The American philosopher Robert Nozick provided another argument against hedonism:[21] suppose that it were possible to be connected to a "pleasure machine" that gave us the happiest feelings imaginable. Would we choose to spend our lives plugged into that machine? His assumption is that most of us would decline, preferring life's rich texture of feelings. This is because the deepest pleasure comes from things that give life meaning and purpose, like our relationships, project, and beliefs.

Nozick's perspective overlaps with that of Aristotle, who made a significant contribution to this debate by questioning the true meaning of pleasure. In particular, he suggested that things are not good or valuable simply because they give pleasure, but rather they give pleasure because we value them. The good life, then, is not primarily about pleasure, but more about what is likely to make life pleasurable or happy. Indeed, the Greek word preferred by Aristotle translates more as "wellbeing" than happiness, carrying with it the idea of active flourishing, rather than passive contentment. In this way, Aristotle developed a fresh perspective on the good life, one in which there was no single necessary or general good, but rather that we should think about issues like pleasure and pain relatively: what is good for one person may not be good for another. It is not then some objective abstract property of things or activities that radiates out wellbeing, but rather the way that we relate to that thing. In essence, Aristotle's conception of the good life was one where we use our faculties and skills to think and act in the best ways possible, according to our value system, coming up with what modern philosophers call our individual "projects." It is based on the application of practical wisdom in everyday life, and not on some kind of rarified intellectual or academic thinking. Aristotle also recognized general situations that bestowed wellbeing and represented the good life, such as that it is better to be free than a slave, better to live in reasonable prosperity than in poverty, better to be talented than not. Through observing such personal and general considerations, we can pursue our version of the good life, leading hopefully to a general sense of fulfillment and perhaps some fleeting periods of happiness.

So, hedonism is also flawed, as reflected in the statement "for what shall it profit a man if he gain the whole world, and lose his own soul?"[22] This remark by Jesus, as recorded in the New Testament, highlights a distinction missing from discussions so far about the good life, a distinction between satisfying one's needs and doing what is right. We do not live by bread alone. The distinction that emerges is between having a good life and leading a good life. To re-phrase it, the good life depends critically on the right "process," as in using our faculties and skills to think and act in the best possible ways. An example is whether we intend to do what is morally good or right, because it is right, and not because it results in some pleasure or wealth. This is "good will," our active attempts to do what is good. It is doing your duty for duty's sake. This may not be the happiest life, but it is more likely to be the worthiest life: a life that is worthy of happiness and which leads to a moral life. I think that this is what Ruskin meant, in saying: "There is no wealth but life."[23] Perceived in this way, the good life is the considered life. According to Socrates, whereas an unprincipled and feckless life is of little real value to the person living it, the thoughtful life is shaped by aims and strengthened by integrity, so that to the fullest extent possible it is lived with purpose, governed by reasoning.

Socrates held that the good life, which he saw as a life lived honorably or rightly, included five virtues: temperance, courage, piety, justice, and wisdom. There are actually many such lists, but these lists alone do not ultimately clarify what constitutes a good life. It was believed by Socrates that it is only through being all that we are capable of being that we can have true self-esteem or feel genuine satisfaction with our lives. This commitment to "excellence" requires self-discipline and a willingness to do limitless work involved in developing oneself. It is an austere and demanding conception of a good life, involving operating with some framework of values and meaning to give orientation and guidelines for life (as in a "good life" road map). An example would be the importance of living in harmony with oneself and with nature. Here are some of the prominent values within philosophical thinking about the good life, including those of Socrates:

- The ideal of harmony (living in accord with nature and the general order of things; appreciating the beauty of life);
- A religious way of life (a way of life that looks beyond the everyday to seek some eternal truth or spiritual guidance);
- The use of reason (the idea that a rational approach enables us to achieve self-mastery and live the intelligent life; the pursuit of truth);
- Self-exploration (a commitment to open-ended exploration of oneself, and a willingness to follow this quest);
- Self-realization (the ideal of authenticity, that is, identifying what is most truly oneself and courageously committing to be true to that self);
- Social involvement (an emphasis on the importance of being with others in a shared social world, as in uniting our resources and sharing our hardships; the pursuit of goodness).

These demanding values can be thought of as representing that "road-map" for a successful retirement, shaping our perceptions of how we should attempt to pursue it, and hopefully minimizing some of the biases, distortions and thinking errors which accompany perception and our efforts at coping.

Plato believed that such virtues were sufficient for the good life, but Aristotle recognized that, although being virtuous was the biggest factor, it did not guarantee happiness. This was because he also recognized the power of luck and the fates in influencing how our life unfolds and how we come to feel about it. For this reason, it is said that the ancient Greeks wished their friends to "do well" and "fare well". Doing well concerned being as virtuous as possible, something that we could actively pursue with a reasonable chance of success, as we can exercise some control. Therefore, to wish someone "does well" is to hope that they will treat others in a virtuous, moral fashion. By contrast, to hope that someone also "fares well" is to recognize that virtue is not enough to deliver happiness: we also need some good fortune. Faring well refers to all those events over which we have no control, whether this is general good luck, winning the lottery, or getting the "rub of the green" through life. For example, you may have worked diligently to make a success of your career, but outside forces conspired against you: your company might have been down-sized or the bottom may have fallen out of your particular market. As Sartre put it, "You are free to try, but not to succeed."[24] Again, the Bible is rich in related views: "I have seen something else under the sun: The race is not to the swift or the battle to the strong, nor does food come to the wise or wealth to the brilliant or favor to the learned; but time and chance happen to them all."[25]

That is, it is possible to live a good life without happiness, but it is not possible to have happiness without also living a good life. Both are necessary conditions for happiness, but success is out of our control, while the good life is within our control, if an exacting philosophy. Although modern life may generally seem to refute this belief, it does appear valid in relation to some scenarios. I am thinking about things like work and sport. In sport, psychologists encourage athletes to distinguish between the goals of "process," "performance," and "outcomes" because attaching too much weight to outcomes (the result) is beyond the athletes control and will inevitably lead to disappointment (e.g. the opposition may be too good, or the referee corrupt). However, the athlete can control how they tackle their sport by disciplined thinking (i.e. through the right process, including appropriate concentration) and skilled action (the performance, including pre-shot routines), promoting a more balanced, sustainable and effective approach (this is picked up again shortly). As the Brazilian footballer Socrates put it (no relation – he was named after the Greek Philosopher): "Beauty comes first, victory is secondary."[26] In work and other spheres of life the truth of this logic is shown by the sad fate of those who gain fame or fortune without disciplined effort or a moral map (e.g. lottery winners). I will return to happiness in the final chapter, to consider modern thinking on happiness. But, I wish to close by noting a paradox: the more we prize happiness, the less likely we are to achieve it: like sleep, it comes to us when we do not seek it, provided we concentrate on adaptive coping (including doing our best with what we can control, and exercising moderation). To make things worse, having sustained happiness as a goal is an unrealistic burden, one which can become a source of chronic misery in itself. As Schopenhauer put it: "There is only one inborn erroneous notion: that we exist in order to be happy."[27]

## Excellence in Life

For Socrates, "excellence" was therefore an integral part of the good life, with engagement in the right kind of "process" the seeming path to excellence. In contrast to such timeless religious and philosophical guidance, modern-day thinkers and therapists have approached aspects of the good life through psychological channels, such as self-exploration and self-realization. A clear example can be found in the world of sport, as per the example of process, performance and outcome goals. This provides a more concrete perspective on being "the best one can be." A large number of books have been written about excelling in sport and I think that we can learn much from these modern glimpses of achieving our full potential. One of my favorites is written by Canadian Terry Orlick.[28] According to Orlick, excellence in sport and in life generally requires us to draw on seven critical elements: an appropriate focus (concentration), suitable commitment (motivation), mental readiness, positive images, confidence, controlling distractions, and continued learning. These are explained shortly, but you may immediately notice some comforting overlap with the reasoning of the ancient philosophers. Orlick likens these seven elements to a wheel, placing "focus" at the hub. He notes how people who are being their best (at anything) are those with skills in concentration. This kind of "self-realization" includes the ability to focus on what one needs to think about at the crucial moment. I will now briefly summarize his points, adding relevant examples.

### Finely Focused

Concentration is the act of directing your thoughts towards a selected task, something we do in a superficial way most of the waking day, like reading these words. However, one reason to think about sport in connection with excellence is because it requires extraordinary concentration, and also because we can see vividly when it breaks down (as in the tennis star, who "chokes" and double-faults). Through attempting to concentrate in sport we glimpse our potential, however fleetingly. We become intensely aware, to the point that we no longer know the thing that previously was so clear. Some activities cultivate or require such deep awareness, like yoga or meditation (see Figure 3.1); others absorb us through their nature, necessitating significant attention to detail (sketching or performing music).

### Motivated

According to Orlick, effort and experimentation are required to find out just what is the most appropriate and helpful focus for a particular activity, and indeed some sport psychologists recommend that a new and suitably specific focus is generated every time. Beyond effort and a willingness to experiment we require "commitment," the motivation to become absorbed

**Figure 3.1**  Developing excellence through self-awareness and discipline

in an action, or to consider the meaning that it provides. Commitment builds on a sense of direction, by for instance refining goals so that they become very clear to us and are frequently recalled. Without such a vision, it is hard to judge whether you are making progress, or to have the necessary drive to improve or make the most of your situation. To illustrate, in sport it might be the goal of reaching a single-figure handicap, whereas in life more generally it may be to make a meaningful contribution to society (e.g. by developing your local museum). Persistence is required and to support this effort Orlick identifies some common motivating forces:[29]

- the sheer enjoyment or love of the activity;
- the sense of feeling fully alive, from being engaged in something challenging;
- the feeling of validation or acceptance;

- the understanding that you are making a difference;
- fulfillment or pride, from performing to the best of your ability; and
- a sense of repaying others for their support or love.

### Really Ready

The next key contributor to excellence is "mental readiness." It means preparing, practicing, training, working, and engaging positively in the necessary effort to achieve excellence. It means building on past efforts by reviewing and evaluating what went well and what requires further attention. Breaking down your grand plan or retirement vision into specifics, so that something useful can be pursued in the very next opportunity, represents this kind of preparation and readiness. It also means identifying those simple joys that are embedded within the effort. Another facet is allowing oneself to recover sufficiently, to have the physical and mental energy to re-engage fully with the effort, itself deeply satisfying.

### Mentally Attuned

The fourth aspect of the excellence wheel is to develop positive visions or images of the performance or outcome that one seeks to achieve. A popular example is the use of visualization, the mental rehearsal of what one is trying to achieve (sport psychologists emphasize that "what you see is what you get"). Of course, our other senses can be harnessed to this positive effort, as in attending carefully to how your muscles feel when you are exerting yourself in some way, or how you perceive your movement while walking (feelization).

### Confident

Confidence is integral to this work, namely the belief that you have the ability to achieve excellence. There are many factors that influence this belief but research has suggested the essence, as summarized in Table 3.1.

### Dealing with Distractions

Reading the points so far, they seem truly exacting and virtually unattainable. Even if you were to have a fleeting experience of being "excellent," you might well expect it to evaporate at the first hurdle. To recognize this

**Table 3.1** Four avenues for improving your self-confidence

| Avenue to confidence | Methods |
|---|---|
| Success (performance accomplishment) | • *Preparatory "routines"* (mental and physical activities that attune you to what you are about to do, such as a "pre-shot routine" in sport). |
| | • *Careful goal-setting* (not just what you aim to achieve, the "outcome goals," but more importantly how you wish to work towards those outcomes – "performance" and "process" goals, like relaxed concentration). |
| | • *Appropriate activation* (e.g. arrange for some rewards for succeeding; and possibly some amusing "punishment" for failing, like wearing a silly hat all day). |
| | • *Systematic and focused technical preparation* (make sure that you have got yourself ready, in terms of any equipment or aids; get the relevant movements or statements perfected (e.g. by setting up some graded simulations, such as rehearsing a speech first in the mirror, then in front of a few friends). |
| | • Ultimately, *ensure success* with gradually more independence ("nothing succeeds like success"). |
| Seeing others succeed (vicarious experience) | • *Watch how other people* who are similar to you in some important way deal with the situation that interests you; study how they handle the situation: which coping strategies might they be using? |
| | • *Systematically imagining yourself succeeding* (or re-playing past successes). |
| You can do it (verbal persuasion) | • Find some appropriate ways of *talking to yourself* before and especially during a challenging task (I like the "normalizing" low-key examples, like: "go to work" or "play the game": basically switching on a well-rehearsed approach as if a pro, without fuss, like another day at the office). This may include finding ways to think differently about a task or challenge (e.g. playing down the importance of the outcome, such as: "there's always tomorrow – just give it your best shot"). Other options, in theory, are to *lower your sights*, so that the task seems easier (e.g. the "less is more" approach; "performance deception"). |
| Feeling good (physiological arousal) | • *Attend to what feels good* in your body – do you have any strength? Any fluidity? Can you feel any nervous energy? Try to recognize the potentially helpful physical and psychological states, treating them as your allies (e.g. re-label "nerves" as "excitement" or "readiness," treating symptoms like butterflies or weak knees as evidence that your system is "green for go"). |
| | • By *emphasizing the positive* you distract from any negatives that might be in your head, but there may be something that is hard to ignore, so treat this sensitively (e.g. try to gradually desensitize yourself to something that was upsetting; during the task, park a worry in a mental "black box," to be addressed at a better time.) |
| | • Once you have got into a positive state, work on maintaining it, especially if things go wrong (e.g. by talking to yourself in calming ways – such as accepting that some setback was unfortunate, but also perfectly reasonable – no one was to blame, it "goes with the territory"; etc.). |

additional challenge, Orlick includes controlling distractions and interferences within his wheel of excellence. Of course, many of the barriers that emerge in relation to our goals are external, due to other people, fate, or life events. However, there are also some crucial internal distractions, as in the occurrence of doubts and worries, ones that can cause you to avoid addressing your goals wholeheartedly. Indeed, avoidance is the most popular coping strategy that people use to deal with anything stressful. It is a very tempting coping strategy when one feels under pressure, uncertain, or simply depressed about the way things are going.

It follows that you can better deal with distraction and obstacles by reducing your stress levels, and by properly apportioning responsibility for any difficulty (thinking straight). You need to try to remain stoical and upbeat (positively preoccupied), persisting with your best efforts, aiming to get as close as possible to your potential.

## Continued Learning

Orlick concludes his "wheel" with a note on the importance of continuing personal development. This reflects the endless journey that is entailed in making the most of our potential, no matter what our level of attainment. To help with this journey, we need to find pleasure in even the smallest things that we do ("magic moments"), drawing out the lessons about what went well, and what in particular it was that we did to make something a success (i.e. the performance and process goals). Other people, such as coaches and educators, thankfully exist to help us with this lifelong learning journey, and they represent a great source of guidance and motivation.

Although explicitly extended to life in general, Orlick's book is mostly about trying to help athletes achieve excellence within sport. However, it does also include material on retirement from sport, and it may be interesting to note his points on the subject:

- Aim to pursue the things that you enjoy doing, the things which have real meaning.
- Respect your choices and try to bring out your best.
- Put yourself in situations where you feel valued, respected, accepted, or loved.
- Focus on things that are in your best interests, and the interests of the people you love.

- Trust your judgment about what is the "right path."
- Respect and help those around you.
- Try to embrace each step down your path.

## Conclusions

Retirement can be a challenging transition, especially if we come to it reluctantly ("unfinished business" or no choice), suddenly (redundancy), in poor health, or worried about our finances. Part of the challenge is to think straight, so that suitable coping strategies are applied. This chapter has stressed the cerebral one of reframing: viewing events in the most positive available light ("every cloud has a silver lining"). This has led us to address the "intellectual capacity" and "purpose" elements in the RECIPE for successful retirement, presented as part of the core challenge of "coping." In Mae's case study we saw several examples of these elements at work in the way she perceived events, helping her to live her version of the good life. I am thinking of her tendency to reframe situations positively, allowing her to engage enthusiastically and to benefit others (e.g. helping her son with his business allowed her to exercise her need to provide social support to all and to "mother" needy students). Athletes are trained to remain "positively preoccupied," constantly reframing setbacks or obstacles. Even the worst of situations can be viewed optimistically, as per Woody Allen: "On the plus side, death is one of the few things one can do just as easily lying down."[30]

If you are retired then you have probably lived long enough to develop your own impressive reframing repertoire. Such perceptions will help you to gain the most pleasure from doing what you want to do. Another example of your ability to reframe comes from research on wisdom. In this sense you might like to think that, although you may be getting older, this has enabled you to acquire some wisdom along the way. This is not abstract philosophy, but "expert knowledge in living." One of the five aspects of this kind of wisdom is the capacity to recognize and manage uncertainty. Related to this is a sound grasp of the available strategies for coping with that uncertainty. Another is a rich understanding about life and how people develop. Such thinking is a priceless resource for effective, resilient coping. This wisdom can help us to "see the wood for the trees" and to recognize crooked thinking and other signs of faulty coping with retirement.

# 4

# Relating in Retirement

We are profoundly shaped by our social world, to the extent that it can make or break us. Perhaps this is because we are the supreme social animal, doing all the things that other social animals do (e.g. cooperating over food and our collective safety), but outdoing them in terms of our commitment to and capacity for "social learning" through observing and imitating other humans. More decisively, we outdo other animals in relation to the extent and nature of human society. The word "society" refers to having colleagues, friends, and allies, people who are joined in civil association, based on organizations from nationhood to sports clubs. Key features are mutual dependence (as it is useful and efficient), a shared identity (including a shared language), complex (hierarchical) organization, and solidarity. If you doubt our unique social status, the complex nature of our social world is illustrated in a well-known book, *The Social Animal* by American Elliot Aronson.[1] This takes a social psychology perspective on humans, considering terrorism, conformity, obedience, politics, race relations, advertising, war, interpersonal attraction, and religious cults.

Social support is therefore critical to thriving, as indicated by occurrences when it is disrupted. When researchers at St Andrews University in Scotland studied the records of over 50,000 married couples in 2010, they noted that 40 percent of men and 26 percent of women die within three years of their partner.[2] Led by Professor Boyle, these researchers concluded that there was "powerful evidence" that, despite other explanations (illnesses, accidents, suicides), it was the loss of the spouse that was primarily responsible for this association. Of course, this "widowhood effect" has been observed informally for centuries, particularly when notable people are involved. For

*The Psychology of Retirement: Coping with the Transition from Work*, First Edition. By D. Milne.
© 2013 D. Milne. Published 2013 by John Wiley & Sons, Ltd.

instance, Britain's former Prime Minister, James Callaghan, passed away aged 92, just 11 days after the loss of his wife of 67 years. The US singer Johnny Cash died at the age of 71, four months after the death of his wife. In short, we can "die of a broken heart": losing a partner had a "robust," adverse effect on life expectancy. The researchers concluded that older people who lose a partner are vulnerable and require social support, especially men, due to their higher statistical vulnerability (which is greater within six months of their loss).

Less dramatic but nonetheless disturbing reactions to the loss of social support are a common finding from research on the effects of retirement, from the study of athletes to the experiences of past US presidents. Sport is especially interesting as, with professional athletes, retirement comes early and the demands of sporting careers can restrict the personal development that might aid coping with transition (i.e. the usual refinement of "life skills" can be disregarded to allow emphasis on physical fitness). According to David Lavallee at Loughborough University, this can be distressing and even traumatic (some 20 percent of athletes require significant psychological help).[3] The reasons include loss of both identity and social support. He evaluated the effectiveness of an educational and supportive approach, featuring self-awareness, transferring skills to new careers, and teaching coping skills. This was supplemented by counseling and other support arrangements. Dr Lavallee provided this program on a one-to-one basis to 32 retired professional soccer players (ex-premiership, in England and Scotland). Compared to a control group, these footballers reported more support and better coping skills, indicating a successful intervention. Specifically, it is thought that these athletes became more confident about their ability to cope with retirement, and enhanced their use of existing sources of social support.

When it comes to past US presidents, the transition to retirement is also problematic, at least for some. The story is told of Franklin Pearce, who seemingly was at a loss once he stopped being US President: "After the White House, what is there to do but drink?"[4] He died of cirrhosis of the liver. George Washington reportedly resumed the management of his plantation and distilled whisky. Some of their peers were more successful in their transition, as in Thomas Jefferson, who built the University of Virginia, as well as inventing furniture items (e.g. the swivel chair). Richard Nixon hardly retired at all: after the disgrace of Watergate (which led to his resignation) he went on to work tirelessly as an author and diplomat, dying in 1994 with his status improved if not repaired (e.g. he was an advisor to his successors, becoming a kind of "elder statesman" for US foreign policy). Subsequently Jimmy Carter and Bill Clinton have maintained the trend of past-presidents who go on to do significant good (e.g. promoting human rights and addressing global poverty). Most recently, George W. Bush suggested that he would be "bored" if he only resumed managing his Texas ranch, so is planning to develop a "Freedom Institute" to promote democracy.[5]

These accounts support the belief that retaining a purpose and social engagement are critical to flourishing in retirement, as included in this book's RECIPE:

Resources (e.g. sufficient money)
Exercise
Coping strategies
Intellectual activity
Purpose
Engagement (social support)

We start with the cornerstone of relating to others considering the importance of a close, confiding relationship, marriage, or other close bonds. I will then introduce a relationship that combines these two ingredients; purpose and social engagement – the role of the grandparent (see this chapter's case study). These relationships are central, but are affected by a number of factors including the place we live and companion pets. The vital thread of "process" that runs through the book is further addressed towards the end of the chapter, in terms of our ability to connect. To illustrate this, I will distinguish between the materialistic emphasis on "having" and the more spiritual emphasis on "being."

## Intimate Relationships

Our greatest social supporters are our partners: surveys indicate that they are the first person we turn to in times of distress, and that their help is highly valued. It is also long-established that being in a close, confiding relationship prolongs our life expectancy (although there remains debate as to whether this is due to couples selecting the "fittest" people or to their fostering "fitness" within marriage). However, the value of this support depends on a viable relationship. How can we ensure that our partner will "be there for us"? Research indicates that couples fare best when they discuss problems openly (being fair and respectful), negotiate shared goals (focus on the future), come up with shared coping strategies (i.e. recognize that both need to change: neither is solely "to blame"), pursue them jointly (as we are both part of a joined-up system), and work through the inevitable trials and tribulations of a married or shared life (resilience). This includes planning for retirement, something that appears to be surprisingly neglected, with the consequence that a crisis can occur once retirement starts. In modern parlance, a "rupture" may occur within the relationship, perhaps because a key issue like the new domestic order was not discussed (especially when one partner retires before the other, but assumes that everything will go on as before). Although regrettable, such ruptures are best viewed as a normal feature of intimate relationships. In keeping with the coping approach, they are stressors, events of limited significance in themselves. What progresses a rupture into something more significant is maladaptive coping, such as avoidance or unhelpful responding (e.g. verbal counter-attacking; physical violence). Therefore, the way forward is adaptive coping by constructive "repair" work (e.g. jointly clarifying assumptions and options). Not only does this overcome the problem, it strengthens the relationship by increasing mutual-support, trust, and problem-solving (another good example of the transactional nature of coping). Various relationship-building therapies underpin these principles (e.g. responding with empathy, rather than anger; recognizing shared responsibility for difficulties).

Of course, sometimes ruptures are too large to repair and couples who were looking forward to spending more time together actually decide to separate. A classic scenario is the couple who planned to retire then open a shop or a bed and breakfast establishment. This can represent a series of difficult stressors, not least having to work together for the first time. Another challenge is preserving solitude, the ability to enjoy one's own company and to obtain pleasure from pursuing activities alone. Far from being a sign of rupture or distress, solitude allows a relationship to "breathe" and the partners to refresh their lives with complementary interests. If repair is impossible, other relationships can take on greater importance, as one needs support and guidance from family and friends during this transition. This will help the grieving process and, perhaps in time, the process of re-engaging with intimate relationships.

The intimate relationships we have in retirement are likely to have weathered the storms of several transitions, as in couples who have survived the trials of child-rearing, adolescent children, mid-life crises, redundancy at work, and so forth. As a result, on the "rupture and repair" logic they will be stronger and better adapted to cope. They are also likely to recognize the importance of relationships in general, and have the time and energy to develop them (e.g. making new friends, investing in family ties). This is a basic building block, a vital resource, sometimes called "social capital." Properly invested, it can make the years of retirement among the best.

As we age our need for support grows, whether for purely emotional reasons or for basic physical ones (e.g. requiring assistance with the tasks of daily living). Of course, for most new retirees in their mid-60s there is hopefully going to be little immediate need for physical assistance. More likely, they will need to adapt to reduced energy, slowed mental performance, lowered self-confidence, or sleep difficulties, seeking to ensure that these do not undermine their supportive relationships. Also, these challenges come at a time when the social support enjoyed at work is lost. If you are one of those who "lived for their work," you may not have invested much in supportive relationships outside work, leaving you socially impoverished once retired: you start your transition to retirement at a disadvantage. If this has included family, there may be some resentment to overcome and bridges to be built.

This line of thinking is supported by a study conducted in Israel in 2009,[6] with over 1,000 workers from the transportation, construction, and manufacturing sectors, with an average age of 58 years. The researchers found that older employees who worked the most approaching retirement, experienced less breadth and depth of support from close family members, and this adverse effect on their close supportive relationships continued once they retired. There was found to be no adverse effect on close (non-work) friendships, and while there was increased *practical* support from former work colleagues, the high work hours were associated with significantly lower levels of post-retirement *emotional* support from these work colleagues. The authors speculated that this was because those working longer hours saw the workplace as their main way of meeting their emotional needs (e.g. for a sense of personal accomplishment or meaning). Retirement may then cause a great sense of loss and a strong sense that the quality of their support has decreased. The authors also noted optimistically that retirement can represent a watershed, a time when we can invest more time and energy in friendships outside work, so compensating for more limited commitments in the past. As a result, emotional support can become adequate once more: a successful adjustment can be made. By contrast, the researchers thought that close relationships take longer to "repair," perhaps because these are not simply a matter of replacing old friends with new ones. In particular, they require the rectification of deficient emotional support that occurred on a daily basis, perhaps because the person working long hours was too emotionally exhausted to reciprocate. A healthy balance is thought to include both partners feeling able to openly share their feelings and emotions, feel respected, receive reassurance when troubled, and trust the other person to be there in times of need. Such emotional support may well have been compensated for by practical support during employment (e.g. dependency on financial benefits), but in retirement some re-balancing is necessary.

In a related study, conducted in The Netherlands in 2005,[7] over 500 couples were asked about the process of adjustment to retirement on two occasions: just before it started and some five years later. The partners in employment worked in Dutch multinational companies in retail, trade, and industry. It is likely that the retirement of one partner will impact the other, even if the other remains in work – both will need to make some adjustments. This might result from reduced household income, disquiet that one person is working while the other is not (for an example, see the case study in Chapter 5), or simply result from the emotional consequences of a changed situation. This rare consideration of the couple as a unit relied on postal questionnaires, completed separately by both partners. The study focused on why some couples adjusted better than others, and what role the partner played in this process. We know from research on illness and disability that the partner can play a highly significant role, but was this also the case with retirement? The authors concluded that their study "provides strong support for the suggestion ... that both the context in which the transition is made and psychological factors are important predictors of difficult adjustment."[8] Two aspects of "context," health and financial factors, were of relatively minor importance in the adjustment to retirement. By contrast, the authors reported that the circumstances (i.e. whether retirement was chosen or imposed) and the retirees' social support were important factors in adjusting to retirement: those older workers who were anxious about the consequences of retirement for their social contacts and social status had greater problems making the transition. This was true regardless of their social position, in the sense that those in relatively menial posts were concerned about the loss of status. Overall, they reported that those with a strong attachment to work, little control over retirement (e.g. redundancy), anxiety about retirement (such as this loss of status), and lower self-confidence struggled most with the transition. What role did the partners play? Surprisingly, partners seemed to exert only limited influence on this experience, something that might link with the earlier point about poor emotional support in the early phase of retirement. Women in this sample tended to have greater problems adjusting to retirement, both as retirees and as partners. The authors thought that there could be two explanations: for women the majority of domestic obligations remained unchanged, so the reality of being a retiree may have been less attractive to women than to men; second, women are normally more open about their symptoms (e.g. pain, depression, or other negative feelings).

In a further study,[9] 32 selected people aged 70 to 80 and living in and around London were asked to complete questionnaires, undergo interviews, and complete activity diaries. Half of these people were selected because they were known to be resilient (i.e. they had overcome adversity and were thriving), while the remaining 50 percent were struggling (based on their reported quality of life). The logic was that by contrasting these separate groups, we might better capture information on what makes a difference to coping. One of the main themes that emerged was that "adversity" mainly took the form of limited circumstances and opportunities, which were brought about by physical, mental, or social losses (e.g. the death or illness of a loved one, ill health, and difficult circumstances). Those who reported struggling to cope reported greater and more complex losses than those with resilient outcomes, such as occupying a long-term caring role or suffering more bereavements. In addition, they experienced more emotionally severe and physically limiting health concerns than the resilient participants. The latter group had better access to social support (i.e. having friends to discuss problems with) and better coping strategies which included reframing adverse events (e.g. not dwelling on setbacks), finding ways to continue in roles and activities that had always brought pleasure, and relying on tried and tested ways of tackling the stressors. This promoted acceptance and distance between the emotional weight of adversity and day-to-day life, though re-adjusting their expectations to changing circumstances.

Sometimes we need support or caring in circumstances where no one is able to help us informally. In such a situation, one of the interesting options in relation to mental health problems is "befriending," where a non-professional volunteer strikes up a regular one-to-one relationship with someone who is lonely or otherwise in need of social support. Research suggests that befriending works, bringing those who require such support, the "befriendees" improved social engagement, higher self-confidence, and enhanced wellbeing. A study of five befriending schemes in London looked at the process with eight befriendees, whose ages ranged from 33 to 57. Using interviews, it appeared that the reasons for these benefits were:

- establishing a relationship (inc. empathy, safety and a sense of tackling problems);
- making sense of events (inc. seeking the meaning within situations- putting things into words and benefitting from a different perspective); and
- promoting change (inc. getting out and doing things; having a healthy relationship).

In summary, retirement is a challenge for retirees and their partners, and some circumstances can be seriously adverse, making it a particularly difficult process. Thankfully, these studies also draw attention to promising coping strategies, like gaining as much control as possible over the circumstances of our retirement, building self-confidence, and strengthening our social support (both at home and through new contacts).

## Partners and Depression: A Research Illustration

The link between marital distress and depression has a strong research foundation, although the nature of the link is complex. Some of the evidence suggests that marital difficulties precipitate depression, but there is also evidence that episodes of depression can lead to marital distress. Whatever the pathway, once one or both members of a couple are depressed, their communication is likely to involve higher levels of negativity and tension, with lower levels of cooperation and problem-solving than their non-depressed counterparts. There is also reason to believe that when we interact with someone who is depressed, we tend to experience a lowering of our own mood, and so naturally tend to try to minimize interaction with that person. However, there is also evidence to indicate the positive effects of relationships as a source of support in coping with emotional distress. Research suggests that the "close confiding relationship" provided by partners is paramount in helping individuals to cope with stressful life events.

However, these opposing forces can create a difficult tension for partners trying to assist their depressed partner, as they need to strike a balance between helping and not being harmed. In one in-depth study,[10] nine couples were interviewed at length about their coping with depression. Their ages ranged from 28 to 57, and their depression ranged from severe to minimal. All were British, coming from "white British" and "black Afro-Caribbean" backgrounds. On average, these participants had been in their relationships for 12 years, and overall they were satisfied with their relationships (although two were confirmed to be in the "marital distress" category). The researcher's believed that a number of themes characterized the couples' attempts to cope with the depression. One of these themes was "bafflement," because the changes that were observed in the depressed partner's mood or behavior were bewildering. Part of this difficulty was explaining the experience of depression to a partner. To make matters worse, because communication was not happening in the normal way, the non-depressed partner presumed that they had done something wrong. Other themes included "battling through" (trying to cope with the depression as a family emergency); coping with the long "grey periods"; "the recovery phase ("starting to swim again"); and "the threat of relapse" as the final theme.

In turn, the participants were asked how they attempted to help one another and again five themes emerged from the interviews: "stumbling along"; "walking on egg shells"; "communication in depression – a catch 22?"; "working together"; and "managing one's feelings as a helper." To illustrate, the "stumbling along" theme referred to the challenging and often confusing experience of trying to cope with the depression. Many of the partners had little idea of how to help and also lacked confidence. Part of the difficulty was that, although the non-depressed partner might be motivated to try and help, the person with depression would typically struggle to say what might be done. These participants had consulted mental health professionals and sought the help of their General Practitioner, and were encouraged to read self-help books and information leaflets. But, these sources of advice and information had been of little practical assistance, and were even "vigorously rejected." This meant that the partners had to work out how they might best cope, often through a difficult process of trial and error. This brought its own dilemmas, in that something that was quite successful one day might lead to a negative reaction the next. As you might imagine, this placed a heavy onus on effective communication and, linked to the "walking on eggshells" theme, even one misplaced word could produce setbacks. However, talking to one's partner is also one of the most valuable ways of managing the depression, creating the "catch 22" theme. Here is what one of the interviewees said: "Talking gets my frustrations and anger out . . . it takes a load off . . . it calms me down . . . you're not quite so on your own. You don't feel quite so isolated. I think you just come out of your hole a bit." [11]

In general, it seemed that the best reaction that the non-depressed partner could give was to provide a message of acceptance: accepting their experience, being receptive and flexible about their needs, and responding minimally and with great care (due to the sensitivity of the depressed person). In essence, it seemed that the best response the partner could give to their depressed partner was almost a counseling style of listening and accepting. This included responding to the "seething mass of emotions" by trying not to react to anger, but attempting to see it as a symptom of the depression.

In summary, these couples' accounts of coping with depression featured a strong sense of bewilderment and struggle, fuelled by powerful emotions. Despite this, the partners were generally resourceful and determined in their support, which was highly valued by the depressed partner. Key features of the support that seemed to help were trust, acceptance, and open communication. Indeed, as the researchers noted, it is as if the qualities that would exist within the relationship under normal circumstances had to be accentuated during the crisis, such as the opportunity to talk about one's experiences, without feeling judged or criticized. If nothing else, this study highlights the importance of including the "nearest and dearest" when thinking about such difficult experiences as depression. It is clear from the above that partners can play a crucial role, shaping the unfolding depression for better or worse, and to do so will also have to dig deep into their emotional reserves. One can imagine that this applies, to a lesser extent, within the wider network of supporters.

## Grandparenting

Another intimate relationship that builds on marriage and long-term relationships is grandparenting. Much has changed in the world of grandparenting. Figures from the US suggest that a century ago only some 20 percent of children had a grandparent by the time they reached the age of 30. Today that figure is around 80 percent. [12] In the UK there are thought to be some 14 million grandparents. These figures reflect the increased life expectancy of older adults, together with a falling death rate among grandchildren (in 1900, 62 percent of children died before the age of 15; by 1976 this had dropped to 4 percent).[13] In addition, a 1998 UK survey suggested that the falling birth rate and growing divorce rate meant that grand-parenting was more likely to be required over an extended period (75 percent of adults become grandparents with the average age of starting to grandparent being 54 years in the UK),[14] and is more likely to represent a substantial role (20 percent of grandparents see their grandchildren at least once a week; 30 percent of grandparents reported seeing their grandchildren several times a week, with a similar proportion seeing their grandchildren less than once a month).[15] Indeed, some people are thought to spend half of their lives in grand-parenting roles, and some grandparents see their grandchildren enter adulthood ("great grandparents").

Another major change has been the hugely-improved status of the grandparent.[16] In the 1930s and 1940s grandparents received a fairly negative press, at least in Western societies. The media presented the grandparent as "aged, fussy, domesticated, sedentary and probably with infirmities."[17] This appears to have some basis in truth, as grandparents have been found to have stricter and more authoritarian views than their children. They were even charged with having a disturbing influence on the children, such that parents were encouraged to protect their children from the malignant effect that some interfering grandmothers had by lecturing the mother on how to rear a child. This can also affect the grandchild's reaction: "I don't like my grandmother; she's sloppy and disagreeable . . . I don't like visiting her"; and "she's always running about, grumbling, nagging and shouting"[18] In response, grandparents have noted feeling trapped in the role, not having enough time for themselves, and lacking privacy. There do, however, appear to be significant exceptions to these views, depending on cultural groups. For example, African-Americans have reported being more satisfied with their grandparenting role, possibly linked to greater social support arrangements.

However, these days it appears that in general, grand-parenting succeeds: "The relationship is usually . . . quite close and satisfying . . . and is seen as positive and important by both generations."[19] Nowadays it seems that grandparents are viewed more favorably, more as a family helpers and confidants than family disciplinarians, perhaps because today's grandparents were themselves raised in more permissive times. Also, today's grandparents are younger than those described above, a description that tends to perpetuate stereotypes that are closer to great grandparents.

Another reason for the current, more favorable view of grandparents has been growing recognition of their valuable role in fostering the

grandchildren's development, not to mention the help that they can provide to their own children's development in supporting and guiding them
to become more effective parents. For example, research indicates that
grandparents transmit positive parenting qualities to the parents, including
warmth, autonomy, affection, and support. In one survey, one-third of the
parents said that they would go to their own mum or dad before they would
approach their friends, the media, or the Internet. Grandparents may also
provide practical and financial assistance. It has been estimated that 30 percent of grandparents put money aside to help their grandchildren to get on
the property ladder.[20] Indeed, in their wills some grandparents bypass their
own children in favor of their grandchildren.

These facts and figures concern well-established families; when something causes a family to shatter, grandparents can play an even more vital
role. Consider the example of a serious drug problem or alcohol misuse
in one or both of the parents: in the UK this has been estimated to lead
to some 200,000 grandparents having their grandchildren living with them
(only a third of fathers and two-thirds of mothers with such problems live
with their children).[21] When grandparents become the primary carers they
appear to have minimal state support, with negative consequences for their
physical and mental health (e.g. depression) resulting from the stress of the
role and the social isolation. Here is a quote from the 2006 report *Forgotten
Families*, by Adfam:

> The loss can't be counted in money terms: loss of our future plans, time
> together, peaceful old age, social life. It's as though someone threw a bomb
> into our lives. But we love our grandchildren dearly; they are beautiful, happy,
> innocent children. Our priority is to nurture and protect them and try, as
> much as possible, to make up for their own awful start in life."[22]

It is also true that grandparents can have a negative effect on children. An
example is through transmitting or condoning traditions of aggressive or
punitive parenting. Similarly, grandparents may also contribute (or damage)
parenting, through the way that they address issues. This includes involvement with childcare, financial support, gifts, companionship/emotional
support, passing on traditions, and the modeling of effective parenting.

As far as the grandchildren are concerned, time spent with the grandparents is typically seen as enjoyable, leading over time to ever closer relationships. An example is the role that the grandparent might play through

conversation, helping the grandchild to understand their family through its history, and by talking about themselves and their experiences in ways that are more problematic for the parents (e.g. children "open up" to grandparents because they may be viewed as safe confidants and because they lack parental authority). For example, a survey of over 1,500 children aged 11 to 16 across England and Wales conducted in 2008 reported that grandparents had considerable involvement in sharing these young people's interests, hobbies and activities, and in talking about their future plans. They also contributed by helping to solve the children's problems (e.g. considering which career to pursue), and by taking part in school activities (e.g. help with homework; cheerleading at school events). In particular, grandparents were recognized as having played a major positive role in some family crises.[23]

Thankfully, this kind of involvement was correlated with a number of wellbeing indicators. It was found that active involvement by grandparents was associated with significantly better adjustment, including fewer emotional, peer relationship, and behavioral problems among the grandchildren. Based on this study, the authors questioned the current low status accorded to grandparents in the UK (e.g. in 44 divorce proceedings, they were viewed as not having an essential purpose or fundamental importance).[24] Rather, they argued that their findings suggested that grandparents played an "important role," providing a vital family buffer that helped to reduce adjustment difficulties arising from adverse life events, especially where a divorce had occurred.

Many adults first become grandparents while they are still actively engaged in their careers and have many other roles and activities. In general, it appears that grandparenting is a satisfying role and indeed the more frequent the interaction between grandparents and grandchildren the more satisfied the grandparents. It appears that this is partly because grandparenting provides a sense of purpose or meaning. It can meet emotional needs (e.g. emotional closeness), create a sense of "immortality" (symbolically, by living on through the grandchild), and allow the grandparent to be a teacher and general helper. This role therefore meets several criteria for "the good life" (see Chapter 3) including feelings of being valued when such needs are greatest (called "generativity"). Just how significant this can become is indicated by the consequences of a break-up in contact (e.g. after a parental divorce) or bereavement. Under such circumstances, grandparents have reported emotional and physical distress (e.g. symptoms of post-traumatic stress, chronic grief, and depression). The loss of a grandchild can provoke even stronger reactions, because it involves the experience of feeling for the grandchild, feeling for their own children – the parents, and managing with their own reactions.

Although we have noted numerous roles, the primary role of the grandparent in Western societies is currently thought to be one of support, the business of being available to help, but not imposing beliefs or attempting to control how the parents behave.

To illustrate the experience of grand-parenting, consider another study based on interviews, conducted in North Carolina in the US.[25] Some 200 men and women, aged between 58 and 64 years, who identified themselves as grandparents and who were still working at least 35 hours a week, were interviewed over the phone. Regarding the grandparenting role, these interviewees gave themselves an average score of 3.4 on a 5-point Likert-type satisfaction scale, indicating that they felt "satisfied" to "very satisfied" with the role. Men and women were both equally satisfied and there seemed to be regular interaction with the grandchildren. However, women seemed to find grandparenting particularly valuable, in terms of its meaning and its role in defining their identity. Specifically, most of the women interviewed ranked the grandparenting role as one of their three most important roles in their life, compared with only 42 percent of the men.[26] This is despite both groups holding similarly positive self-images, and not differing in relation to their self-esteem. Some social background factors did appear to play a role. The researchers found that being married was positively related to contact with grandchildren for grandfathers, whereas education was negatively associated with contact for both grandmothers and grandfathers. White grandfathers had less contact with their grandchildren than did black grandfathers, in this sample. Another factor was poor health, which was positively related to the amount of contact with grandchildren for grandmothers, but negatively related in the case of grandfathers. The researchers thought this might be due to grandchildren initiating more contact during periods of poor health, out of a sense of sympathy or obligation, especially for their grandmothers. Another explanation is that contact with grandchildren may be perceived as a firm expectation as part of a woman's role in Western society. That is, contact with grandchildren becomes a right and proper behavior for women, regardless of their grandparent identity or the centrality of the grandparenting role. In contrast, the grandfather's role may contain fewer expectations and is generally more voluntary than for women. Emerging from this detailed analysis was the expected finding: the more frequent the contact between grandparents and grandchildren, the more satisfied grandparents with the role.

## Case Study: John and Kate Love Visiting Grandson Frank

John had retired at the age of 65, several years ago, and his wife Kate had retired at 60, 13 years previously. This made them relatively old grandparents when their one and only grandchild, Frank, was born, six years ago. Another limiting factor was that they live hundreds of miles from their child, so could usually only manage one visit to Frank's home each year.

John likes to keep himself busy, enjoying gardening and working on things in the garage ("you've never seen anything like it"). Kate used to have a busy social life, but a recent road traffic accident has resulted in some memory problems and difficulty walking.

In this context, young Frank is a "joy," someone with whom they can spend time reading books highlighting for them how "delightful" a child he is: "hard work, but we love it" (see Figure 4.1). John spoke with pleasure about how they would walk into town together: "when we get to the cross-roads, his little hand will come up and look for mine – just lovely." Frank also makes them laugh, as when he comes into their bedroom and says: "well I'm awake – what about you?" or rushes in to take an embarrassing photo. When prompted, they could readily recognize a wish to help Frank to develop (generativity again), giving the example of social skills: "As an only child, we want him to be willing to wait his turn, but also not too shy to take his turn, and to share fairly." They also noted that there are "so many books to read" for school.

In terms of supporting Frank's parents, John and Kate take definite plea-sure in being able to care for Frank, so that his parents can go out socially, or go for a jog together. There was clearly a sense of mutual benefit, as coming to visit was itself a welcome change, and it was "a joy to help them (Frank and his parents), and to help ourselves – give and take." In effect, "Frank draws us all together as a family . . . for example, Frank will phone and invite us up: "you do realize you can come and stay, any time." As well as "feeding us for a week," such calls help John and Kate to feel part of the community of grandparents. They have lots of family and school photos

**Figure 4.1**    Grandparents help children to develop, a profoundly satisfying experience

on display at home, which are a source of deep pleasure: "lovely to look at, and realize: what a lovely little fella." When together, the grandparents are accorded due authority: "When Mum's not here, you're in charge, aren't you Gran."

## Companion Pets

In addition to the companionship that they provide, pets ease the path to social support. They can also help us to feel better, physically and emotionally, which can aid us in getting the best out of ourselves and our relationships. A case in point is the vets, which (as already noted) can be a setting for emotionally-loaded interactions. Consider a small personal project that studied 100 consecutive clients attending a vet's surgery,[27] half of whom were at least 65 years old. We observed the vet's social support interactions with his clients and also asked the clients to complete a social support questionnaire. This asked questions like: "To what extent can you talk about a specific problem with the vet" (and a range of other potential supporters, such as "partner"). Although we did not find any difference between the older and younger clients, we did find that the vet provided significantly more emotional support to the older adults. The questionnaire findings supported this as the older respondents reported receiving significantly more social support. This extended beyond "emotional" support to "socializing" (companionship), and to practical and informational support. Indeed, for these older clients, socializing was judged to be the main function served by the vet's support, whereas the younger clients regarded the practical assistance as the main function. Research in the US has furnished similar findings, indicating a positive social support bias towards older adults.[28] When we asked our vet about this, he said that he felt a special responsibility towards the older clients.

It appears that we can get very attached to our pets, a bond built on the unconditional love that they can give, our caring for them, and the security or protection that they can provide. The depth of this bond is indicated by a study of bereavement reactions following the death of a pet.[29] A survey of 88 people who had lost their pets highlighted a reaction directly comparable to the loss of a loved one: initial numbness and disbelief; preoccupation with the loss, and feelings of anxiety and depression. Furthermore, those owners who had perceived their pets most intimately (e.g. as their "baby") reported the worst grief reactions, whereas those who regarded their pet as more of a friend experienced fewest bereavement symptoms. Interestingly, these reactions were linked to the adequacy of the owners' social support: where the pet served as a major form of support (e.g. as a "companion"), reactions were worst. The authors concluded that the bereavement reaction only really differed in terms of the extent of the reaction, being weaker for pets.

In terms of our health, pets have long been thought to bring benefits.[30] In the extreme case of the old, what were then termed, "lunatic asylums" sheep, hares, monkeys, and other domestic animals were routinely part of these establishments, as they were thought to foster "a less hostile and more attractive environment ... encouraging benevolent feelings."[31] In other hospitals Florence Nightingale noted that patients confined to the same room gained pleasure from the presence of a bird. More recent research has generally indicated that animals benefit our health, as indicated by these preliminary findings:[32]

- Dog owners are nearly nine times more likely to still be alive one year after a heart attack.
- Cat owners have a 30 percent lower risk of death from a heart attack.
- Pet owners are significantly less likely to develop coronary heart disease than those that do not own a pet owners.
- Blood pressure is reduced when watching fish swimming in a tank (while doing a stressful task); heart-rate drops in the presence of a dog.
- Companion pets can help to reduce anxiety and depression following a major life event (e.g. divorce; bereavement) and foster feelings of competence and self-esteem.
- Swimming with dolphins lowers anxiety.
- "Animal-assisted therapy" improves behavioral problems and various medical difficulties.

As to why pets have such effects, it has been suggested that this is due to their companionship, greeting rituals, affectionate nature (e.g. the act of stroking), loyalty, and capacity to aid us (e.g. guide dogs), the protection they provide, and (particularly in times past) to help provide food for us. This is in addition to the way that they can reduce our symptoms of stress (as detailed above), encourage us to exercise, and facilitate social support. Latterly there has been interest in the capacity of some dogs to detect health problems, such as alerting their owners to imminent epileptic seizures or hypoglycemic episodes. Of course, different animals have different strengths, but this helps to explain why "a dog is a man's best friend."

## Conclusions

Retirement is one of life's major transitions, which is partly because it disrupts social support (e.g. through leaving our colleagues), leading to reduced socializing and to a general reduction in the kind of structured activity that work provided. This places a big onus on the intimate relationships that we maintain with our family and friends, as well as on the more fleeting but still vital forms of social support that we get from our neighborhood. Whether from intimate relationships or not, effective social support includes informational, practical, and emotional help, and provides general companionship. It gives us a sense of attachment, belonging, recognition, and guidance.

It appears that there are many ways in which we can develop effective relating in retirement, and, in this chapter I have considered ways of repairing the inevitable ruptures that characterize a healthy, vibrant relationship. Being a grandparent is another distinctive and positive role that can be available in retirement, one that usually bestows advantages on all concerned. Companion pets also appear to play a valuable role in managing the retirement transition. They may strengthen links between people, while also providing a sense of emotional closeness that at times rival our human relationships. Out of these comforting social resources we can replace the support we received at work, creating a vital sense of belonging, commitment, and purpose.

# 5

# Supporting Retirement

As discussed in the last chapter, we are by nature highly social animals. It is not surprising, then, to find that the social support we experience relates closely to all kinds of health indicators. Indeed, it seems that social support can carry as powerful an effect as a history of smoking or a high cholesterol level (though in opposite directions: social support has a positive effect). This important role seems to be amplified in situations where people encounter difficulty in their lives, such as those experienced on 9/11:

> People expressed many different reactions to the events of September 11th, 2001. Some of these reactions were clearly negative, such as political intoler-ance, discrimination, and hate crimes ... other reactions were more positive. For example, people responded by donating blood, increasing contributions of time and money to charity, and flying the American flag.[1]

Although there is reason to believe that as we get older we are content with smaller social networks, this does not appear to alter the importance of having *adequate* social support. That is, it is the quality of social support that matters, as measured by its capacity to meet our basic social needs (for a sense of belonging, an emotional connection, etc.).

This chapter builds on the material in the previous chapter by exploring a fascinating range of support situations that are of special relevance to retirees: social support, where we live, tourism, and religion (and related spiritual activities). Aside from these topics, a significant difference between this chapter and Chapter 4 is that we now consider the wider social world: the things that surround or embed the intimate relationships and support discussed in Chapter 4. In this sense, we move on from the personal to

*The Psychology of Retirement: Coping with the Transition from Work*, First Edition. By D. Milne.
© 2013 D. Milne. Published 2013 by John Wiley & Sons, Ltd.

the social, from partners to friends, from grand-parenting to religion, from pets to places and travelling. These are some of the key factors that can be thought of as nourishing or enabling personal support, giving it the necessary context and meaning. The common denominator for both chapters remains adaptive coping, and Gareth in the case study is a prime illustration of how we can adapt to retirement successfully, suggesting what we can do to try to ensure that we continue to receive adequate support. Reflecting this logic, I will start with the most vital and immediate aspect of personal relationships, the social support that we receive from our friends and community. Next I will give these social processes a basis, by considering the role played by the places in which we live. In an important sense, we only truly know our home and community by comparison with the alternatives: by heightening our awareness of just what it is that makes us consider a place as special, as home, and by contrasting this with other places. The saying "who knows England, who only England knows?"[2] in my mind demonstrates the benefits of this comparison. Travelling is therefore an appropriate topic, and I will pose my own question: why do we do it? An improved understanding of our motives in travelling may enhance the experience, better meeting our support needs. Lastly I will consider religion and spirituality, giving some depth to my recommendations for retirement. In terms of my retirement RECIPE, the emphasis will be on "engagement," with some attention also to "coping strategies" and "purpose" (see Chapter 1).

## Social Support

For most of us, our social world is built on close, confiding relationships that provide vital emotional support and a sense of attachment. We all need regular contact with family and friends to stay balanced. The term "social support" captures this aspect of our lives, consisting of *emotional, practical,* and *informational* help, plus general *companionship*. We can think of social support as a resource, something that supplements our personal coping strategies (it is sometimes called 'social capital').

Although phrased positively, it is of course recognized that each of these forms of support can also be problematic. Such is the complexity of our social world that we also need to acknowledge the difficult social interactions that can undermine our coping efforts and lower our morale. A classic example is where well-intentioned parents give negative emotional messages to their child, by criticism and over-involvement. Another example is where a person offers first-rate social support to a friend, but, in doing so, encourages dependency: the friend relies excessively on the support, routinely "off-loading" many of their difficulties, resulting in the supporter becoming overwhelmed by someone's chaotic and confused world. Other types of "*anti*-social support" are disapproval, excessive emotionality (e.g. creating anxiety), the lack of reciprocity (e.g. making someone feel indebted or inadequate), emotional distancing ("cold-shouldering"), and routinely challenging or questioning someone's actions (undermining or belittling). In the worst circumstances, *anti*-social support can erode our interest in people and drive us to despair.

More commonly, people relate to others in a far more supportive manner, with profound results. Specifically, social support fosters a sense of *attachment*, enabling a relationship to become closer, with mutual nurturing, assistance, and a shared sense of safety or trust. It also tends to strengthen the sense of *belonging*, the feeling of being part of a couple, group, or culture, which gives a sense of *integration*. It additionally promotes *recognition* and helps to validate individuals (e.g. appreciating their skills, values or knowledge). It strengthens the sense we have of our personal *identity* and *enhances self-esteem*. It can help us to manage or *regulate feelings* (e.g. by enabling people to "ventilate" their negative feelings and encouraging positive feelings). And finally, social supporters help by *guiding* how we cope, as in suggesting refinements to our approach, indicating alternative interpretations of events, or offering feedback on our coping efforts. As a result of receiving some or all of these forms of support, we are buffered from stressors, our coping repertoire is strengthened, and self-esteem is boosted. Although family and friends are the primary sources of support, wherever people interact, social support can be seen to be operating. The quote from the article on 9/11 above can be seen to touch on several of the functions of social support. A clear everyday example is the local community, with the High Street a rich source of support. For instance, studies of hairdressers suggest that this is actually their main role, approximating to informal counseling[3] Similarly, vets and their assistants provide compassion and caring when pets are ill. Florists encourage customers to indicate the happy or sad reasons for their visit (special occasions, funerals, etc.) and so it goes on. Through these and many other instances, our communities afford us with the opportunity to interact with others and, in doing so, receive social support. This may well be weaker and less helpful than the support we get from partners and family, but it complements and enriches that help.

Therefore, an appropriate term for such resources is "social capital." This includes your available network of supporters, and also what is deemed "normal" in relation to support within each group: the degree to which you can each trust and help one another. With greater social capital we will act together more effectively, responding jointly to adversity and towards shared goals, in ways that tend to promote heart-warming things like reciprocity, social bonds (cohesion), belonging, meaning, and purpose. Building such capital can be problematic, it is not always easy for us to seek inclusion in groups unknown to us and some find this to be difficult; however, special interest clubs, befriending and mutual support groups can make a real difference. Gareth's retirement experience, described in the case study below, illustrates these points. Next I will discuss places, because of the role that they play in providing a platform or stage on which social support occurs.

## Knowing One's Place

A distinct community platform for social interaction is the university, a civil association which specializes in promoting knowledge. When making his Address to Glasgow University in 1972, new Rector Jimmy Reid highlighted our need for social support by criticizing "alienation."[4] This refers to how individuals experience despair, hopelessness, and disengagement from society. Jimmy Reid also referred to some people becoming dehumanized by capitalist society. In this sense, even the most "successful" people can become alienated: "It partially de-humanizes some people, makes them insensitive, ruthless in their handling of fellow human beings, self-centered and grasping ... they are losers. They have lost essential elements of our common humanity. Man is a social being. Real fulfillment for any person lies in service to fellow men and women."[5] Jimmy Reid illustrated this alienation by commenting on the so-called "rat-race," inherent in the phrase "look after number one." He continued: "To the students I address this appeal. Reject these attitudes. Reject the values and false morality that underlie these attitudes. A rat race is for rats. We are not rats. We are human beings."[6] These words remain true today, thus supporting the notion of "the good life" discussed in Chapter 3: we are social beings and providing support can bring profound fulfillment.

In addition to the emotional distancing of alienation, physical distance between family members is known to affect social support, but generally we pay little heed to the role played by locations. Therefore, you might be surprised by the degree to which the physical characteristics of the places we live in or visit affect our interactions with others and the level of social support. The ancient Greek philosophers knew this, commenting that places play a part in creating "the good life," recommending "loving country life." Within a town or city, the way that planners arrange the streets, neighborhoods, and buildings will affect opportunities for social engagement. It appears that the right degree of proximity promotes social interaction and support: greater contact between people generally reduces hostility and fosters mutual liking, understanding and trust. Other important aspects of places are the privacy and autonomy that they provide: U-shaped courts, protective fences, shared access stairs, smaller numbers of houses or flats, better lighting, cul-de-sac streets, and common play areas tend to enhance the residents' sense of belonging and the availability of social support. The same principles apply to public parks and shopping centers, but it is vital to find out how the people in such settings perceive these various features, rather than assuming that they automatically foster support.

Places are important for other reasons. We all live in an environment with a certain degree of personal space, whether a high-rise flat or a country manor. However, this is not the same as the concept of "place" or "country," a notion implying that a space has a special meaning, related to specific emotions for an individual or a group (as illustrated by the 9/11 quote at the start). There are actually few aspects of the things that really matter to us that are not connected to places. This "place attachment" is an emotional bond between a specific spot and an event, pleasant or unpleasant. There are many pleasant examples to be found in music: think of "Finlandia," the classical music tribute by Sibelius to his homeland. There are equally many examples of unpleasant associations in music: in blues music, for instance, concerns of persecution are an inherent factor of this musical genre (e.g. "Alabama Blues" by J.B. Lenoir)

As these examples indicate, the emotional associations with a place can be deeply felt. At the positive end of the spectrum we may feel attached to a place, we can be said to have an emotional connection to a familiar and liked location, perhaps our own neighborhood or town. This is usually based on a strong sense of belonging, a sense of being embedded, of having "roots" in the place. Such a feeling is most likely to come from having spent much of our lives in a familiar, much-loved location: we develop a "place identity." For instance, someone might say that their home town "has become a part of me." Similarly, a common question when we first meet someone is: "Where are you from?"

Conversely, one might feel detached from a place, and experience a strange discomfort or even alienation, as often occurs when people first migrate to somewhere new. Such negative place identities can have surprisingly powerful effects on our self-esteem, confidence, and sense of identity. This seems to arise from the way that we draw on the ties we have with a place (and especially with the people we are familiar with there) in order to build a sense of belonging. For instance, it appears that when emigration goes wrong, there is both a disruption to place attachment and a threat to individual identity. This seems to arise because the changes that occur through emigration stretch and even break the bonds that exist between a person and familiar locations. Part of the problem is that these bonds are not normally recognized, being an automatic link and something that is taken for granted. As a result of such disruption, it is not uncommon for those who emigrate (or in other ways are removed from a positive identification with a place) to experience anxiety and loss. In this sense, one can begin to see how a retirement plan that involves relocation abroad can backfire, with the loss of place identity plus the loss of social support.

For those with the desire and the income, a positive move into some kind of retirement community may appeal, offering an attractive lifestyle, new social ties and appealing resorts or facilities. According to data from the US Census, 10 percent of people choose to relocate when they retire,[7] though the great majority wish to stay put. A key consideration in selecting a seductive new retirement landscape is whether relocation compounds or corrects your social support status. One can see that escaping abroad to an attractive climate (and far from an adverse social situation) has its appeals, and there may seem to be little to lose. However, it is all too easy to underestimate the support we take for granted in the familiar location in which we live, not least the comforting effects of familiar surroundings, routines, and facilities. By contrast, your social capital in a new environment will be very limited, the stressors of making the transition considerable (and often underestimated), and you may be surprisingly homesick. This distressing condition features feelings of longing, dread, grief, yearning, and possibly separation anxiety, a sense of helplessness at the dislocation, social withdrawal, or even depression. These feelings may mirror those of bereavement. Homesickness results from the loss of familiar places and people, the experience of not "belonging" somewhere, of feeling "dislocated" and uncomfortable in oneself (unattached, depersonalized). Familiar music, books, and of course maintaining as much long-distance contact as possible with friends and family may relieve this uncomfortable state. If possible, tackling relocation gradually helps, as does the passage of time, especially if this time is filled with positive efforts to integrate into the new culture (e.g. building up a new support network, including at least one close relationship). For those who stay at home we should recognize that fresh challenges are a great stimulus, providing the brain with problems to solve, which is very important for continued wellbeing. It seems that the critical issue is one of balance, of staying within your comfort zone while addressing the need for support, continuity, novelty, and so on.

Of course, many moves are forced upon us by circumstance. As time passes, the likelihood is that the need for help (with the activities of daily living) or financial strains will make relocation necessary for many. For instance, according to the US Census, 13 percent of those aged 65 to 69 reported a functional impairment, increasing to 28 percent for those over 79.[8] In the developed countries, it is a sad truth that caring for a close family member will often be arranged through professional supporters (e.g. relocation to a care home or other form of "assisted living"). Other cultures are perhaps more considerate. A striking account of this contrast appeared in a letter to *The Independent*, written by Richard Lyon who stated:

> I married an Eritrean woman and over her dead body would her parents be placed in the care of others if a time ever arose when they could no longer manage by themselves. As the eldest of three siblings it will fall to her, and our household, to take in either parent should this scenario ever arise. I believe that this is pretty much a universal attitude in African nations, where elders are respected, revered and cared for. To people from such cultures, the British way of packing off their parents to homes is unfathomably cold and uncaring.[9]

To continue with the subject of "belonging," a further example can be seen in the "not in my back yard" (NIMBY) phenomenon, which is often used to explain public opposition to developments near our home or community, such as the creation of wind farms. NIMBYs are residents who are emotionally invested in their places and so want to "protect their turf." They have protectionist attitudes and adopt oppositional tactics as a community when faced with unwelcome neighborhood developments. They will tend to perceive these developments as necessary but not acceptable near their own homes or communities. In one study in Wisconsin, researchers noted a number of "place protective" actions by residents, including voting for new laws and joining protest groups. It appeared from this research that this opposition was based on a strong attachment to the place, including the sense of meaning that was given to it.[10] The term NIMBY is pejorative, characterizing the opponents of neighborhood developments as self-centered and irrational.

Against this view, others have noted that a NIMBY stance may be based on exceptionally good information, together with rational arguments revolving around justice, equity and trust.[11] NIMBYism also represents a response when our attachment to a place is threatened, including a threat to our identity. An example is where a new energy project is seen to be destructive to the distinctive features of the environment, as when a wind farm introduces alien features that overwhelm the local character of the area, possibly even stigmatizing it. In this sense, unwelcome sights, smells, and sounds may feel threatening, destroying cherished local places. Psychologically, the inability of NIMBYs to prevent developments, despite engagement in public consultations, can undermine confidence and create anger as the new technologies may be felt to have been imposed by large companies or even governments without genuine public consultation, undermining the sense of personal and territorial control in those who feel strongly emotionally attached to their "place."

Researchers have noted that the coping strategies of those opposing major environmental changes cause disruption and the NIMBY phenomenon can involve social support, where individuals communicate concerns to trusted others through their local networks, helpfully sharing emotions and attempting to understand ongoing processes. Alternatively, individuals may engage in political action, developing petitions, write letters to their political representatives, and engage in some form of collective protest. A popular personal coping strategy is to re-interpret the change in the most positive light possible (reframing), particularly once it is impossible to stop a development. Of course, those who are able to do so may simply escape, through selling up and moving on. Whether you like them or not, NIMBY groups may be seen as promoting social capital through public consultation, strengthening the sense of personal involvement and of territorial control; or conversely, they can be accused of undermining mutual confidence within a community and of generating anger. Whatever your perspective, the NIMBY phenomenon illustrates how strongly we can feel about "our patch," and how this is linked to the social support of shared emotions and collective action.

More dramatically, when an environmental disaster (flood, earthquake, etc.) demolishes homes and neighborhoods, major psychological complications arise (possibly exaggerated by intergroup conflict). It appears that the extent to which we become anxious about such disruptions will vary depending on how dramatic the change is, how quickly it happens, how much we feel we have control over it, and our ability to make sense of and cope effectively with the unfolding events. Other feelings that have been noted in relation to disrupted place attachment include "emotional volatility," which is a progression from feelings of shock and denial to feelings of anger and depression. Processes like social support and effective personal coping can, with disaster relief services in place, result in the stress becoming more manageable with the gradual acceptance over time of major environmental changes. A case in point was 9/11, a major terrorist attack which challenged how Americans understood their cultural world, provoking moral outrage and leading to strenuous social efforts to affirm shared values and ideals, amongst other intense reactions:

> Americans drew closer not only to friends and loved ones, but also to their fellow citizens . . . Everybody on the street was talking to each other . . . making sure everybody had a place to go . . . it was kind of cool the way New Yorkers really came together.[12]

Surveys following 9/11[13] indicated that 60 percent of Americans felt that their personal relationships were stronger than one month before the attack, and trust in fellow citizens increased by 10 percent. However, it appears that those who responded to the attack with high levels of moral outrage (i.e. vilifying those responsible and seeking revenge) found it hard to achieve "closure." By contrast, those who coped by focusing on how decent people can be (through volunteering to help, donating time and money to charity, giving blood, etc.) were better able to achieve closure.

Before leaving the subject of places, we should acknowledge the role that the right location can play in boosting our general quality of life. While it has long been recognized that exceptionally beautiful places can inspire awe or give us a sense of perspective, such as walking in a forest or climbing a mountain, it does not require such magnificence to foster a feeling of a good quality of life. One small but interesting study concerning this was based on interviews conducted in 1999 with 16 Chinese people.[14] The males and females selected represented older adults (50–65 years) and a younger group (20–35), from urban and rural locations. Their replies suggested that their housing was a core contributor to their quality of life, not only giving shelter but also regarded as a place that creates the basis for marriage, where the family comes together, or where friends can visit. Here is a quote from one of the interviewees:

> I did not marry my husband until we purchased a flat. This flat is a place completely belonging to us; it represents the existence of our family. It gives us a sense of a home to return to. If I had not had the flat, I would feel that I do not have a home.[15]

A house was therefore perceived as a private place, one's own space, somewhere to recover from the anxieties of public life. Linked to housing was a particularly Chinese notion, "fengshui," which refers to beliefs about where we should build our homes, how we should arrange our internal space, and even how we relate to nature. For instance, care is taken to select the "right" site for a house, to ensure that the family who live there live a happy and peaceful life (e.g. south-facing and surrounded by green mountains and rivers). A further factor is building near one's ancestors, which is thought to increase the sense of having "roots" in a location. In Chinese culture, social connections (membership of a community) follow from observing these considerations, creating a sense of meaningful social existence, as in fostering mutual support. These views seemed to be shared by all interviewees, as the authors did not distinguish between the different age groups. The following case study gives further examples of the importance of place.

## Case Study: Gareth the Gardener

Gareth retired from a career in the National Health Service (NHS) 13 years ago, at the age of 60. He had always worked full-time and was a very busy and dedicated clinician, with the added challenge of managing other NHS staff. Following his retirement he gradually reduced the time he gave to post-retirement work over a nine year period. This new work was a variety of consultancy and part-time clinical teaching that continued his professional interests (e.g. writing clinical reports, research supervision, teaching, and marking students' assignments). This continued until four years ago, by which time he was down to a day a week: "I gradually scaled down until a new professor arrived and then, when I could see some old ideas and mistakes recurring, it seemed time to leave."

This gradual reduction in work while maintaining well-established skills is highly consistent with the collective wisdom on coping with retirement. When asked how he felt his own retirement was progressing he was upbeat: "I feel very fortunate ... healthy and financially OK ... coping ... quite enjoying retirement ... don't worry about it." In addition to this gradual approach to retirement another rather unusual aspect of Gareth's adjustment was that he drew on his skills as a developmental psychologist to manage the transition. This way of looking at how life unfolds helped him to take a different attitude to the retirement experience, one that perhaps helped him to understand himself and some of the changes that were unfolding. An example was a growing awareness of forgetting peoples' names. He addressed this by monitoring his memory, but with a relative acceptance that this is a normal part of growing old: "I don't go rushing off to the doctor: I accept the problem and work on prevention."

Another example that Gareth gave of a coping strategy was in relation to his physical problems (such as backache and a knee problem, due to gardening). Rather than seeking a medical treatment, he managed by seeing a physiotherapist then taking some preventive action. Gareth gave other examples of the coping strategies he uses to maintain his wellbeing in retirement: he kept a diary to record observations of changes in his health; and he thinks that his professional expertise in developmental psychology made him "more accepting ... don't get so angry," encouraging a more positive attitude in which he accepts responsibility and acknowledges that partial loss is part of the normal course of events.

Seeking to maintain key aspects of working life in this manner is a recognized part of successful retirement, contributing to that cherished goal of "meaningful activity" and helping to keep as many parts of life as constant as feasible. Gareth also developed diverse hobbies, including gardening (through renting two local council allotments); attending seminars in the local university history department; eating out and watching films; undertaking voluntary laboring work in a local park; visiting London exhibitions; and travelling (particularly linked to an interest in archaeology, shared with his wife). Gareth also viewed it as "very important" to develop new skills in the first three years after retiring, particularly attending classes in order to learn how to use a computer for email, report-writing, browsing the Internet, and so forth. He said that "the willingness to get wised-up is crucial and it saddens me to come across so many retired people who refuse to have anything to do with computers."

## Allotments

If we focus on Gareth's hobby of gardening in the allotments, it appears that this helps meet his personal need for social support. To quote extensively from Gareth's emails regarding the matter, he noted the "rich variety" of the people who had neighboring allotments, including some younger families and people from Asian and Caribbean backgrounds, making for "an interesting diversity (not the least in terms of what they grow)." These people also varied in terms of their work histories, some coming from local industry, and quite a number were self-employed tradesmen. There were also prison officers, policemen, firemen, and teachers. Gareth felt that some had suffered in terms of the "huge toll on their health" that was exacted by their work: "I'm surrounded at the allotments by a lot of friends who have had strokes, multiple heart attacks, as well as hip and knee replacements: it makes me feel very fortunate." For some, "retirement couldn't have come too soon." Some of the people had sad stories to tell, often linked to the demise of local industry "which just vanished within the space of a decade, and in the worst and most awful cases their pensions were lost as the companies went bust." Diversity within the allotments included variable financial status, differing health conditions, and wide-ranging ethnic backgrounds. Despite this, the wisdom that is shared among the plot holders when someone is approaching retirement is to "try to scale down gradually and just wait and see, without getting over-committed."

In Gareth's view, there are other intrinsic benefits to maintaining an allotment, including the satisfaction of growing one's own produce and using economical resources to reap good crops. Some of the plot holders seem to have replaced working life with allotment life, in that Gareth reckoned that the average time needed to keep a plot up to scratch would equate to some 6 or 8 hours per week, but some plot holders spend nearly as many hours on their allotment daily. This may partly be for rehabilitation reasons (e.g. to help recovery after surgery), but it seems that this commitment may also have a general positive effect on wellbeing, through the involvement in such peaceful, constructive activity among like-minded others, out in the fresh air (see Figure 5.1). There is also the sense that the allotment is a practical challenge, where people can exercise problem-solving skills, leading to several benefits. One example that Gareth gave was a man who was forced out of business after having a stroke, one that resulted in speech and memory difficulties and in him using a mobility scooter to travel to and from the allotment. This man began work on the allotment a year or so ago and was

**Figure 5.1**    The allotment as place for recovery, meaningful activity, and social support

supported by his family. His son had helped to create some raised beds and access paths to enable his father to make best use of his patch of land. This man is now to be found on his plot most days of the week, partly as he believes that it has worked wonders for his speech and general physical fitness. As an example of problem-solving, he is proud to have built his own miniature trailer for his mobility scooter. Gareth's own experience is similarly positive, although he counts his blessings that he has not had to endure any significant physical illness: "I enjoy labouring outside, and at home we enjoy eating our own home grown produce. It is a very social activity, and I find that it is particularly enjoyable because it brings me into contact with a rich variety of people."

*Making Sense of It All*

In conclusion, it did seem to both Gareth and I that his stimulating range of retirement activities served the priceless purpose of maintaining balance in his life, as well as in the lives of his wife and wider family. He stressed that his marriage was close, including clear agreement on "how we do retirement," each following their own "journey," but always sharing experiences, discussing who they had met, what they had done, and so on: "hugely important, but the sort of shared experience that can come under stress in the event of illness, etc." When asked whether his retirement marked a transition to something new and different or the continuation of familiar activities, he tended to agree it was the latter. For example, he remained "extremely busy," a definite characteristic of his earlier professional life. In addition, one can see that maintaining established hobbies affords Gareth meaningful activity, as interest in history keeps alive many long-standing traditions surrounding his childhood, his parents, and his culture. One gains a sense that Gareth is cocooned within family tradition, providing him with a comforting sense of stability and continuity.

## Tourism

A popular activity for new retirees is travelling, and the case study of Gareth included travelling linked to an interest in archaeology, shared with his wife. He is not alone. In general, senior citizens in developed countries often possess the wealth, the time, and the fitness to engage in extensive travelling. Indeed, many are willing to spend a significant amount of their savings on travel, including frequent trips abroad where they traverse long distances and spend long periods away from home. What do retired people actually do when they travel, and why do they do it?

In one study, a mail survey was sent to almost 300 independent male and female Israeli retirees, aged 50 or older, and who had travelled abroad at least once in the year preceding the survey (conducted between 2007 and 2008).[16] The average age of this group was 66 years, 62 percent of this group was female and the great majority were married (79 percent). These participants listed a considerable number of activities that they engaged in when they reached their vacation destination, including: visiting parks, forests or protected lands; visiting towns and villages; spending time next to the sea or a lake or a pool; and walking or biking, in nature. These activities were grouped together under the heading "back country" activities. By contrast, another cluster of activities were treated as "educational" (i.e. visiting places of historical interest, sightseeing in big cities, and visiting galleries or museums). A third cluster of activities were termed "city-based" and involved visiting coffee shops, restaurants, shops, markets, and night clubs. By contrast, another group were interested primarily in physical activities such as exercising, gym, ball games, or visiting health spas. The "cultural" sub-group of tourists preferred to spend their time watching the performing arts, (attending local festivals, or getting to know local people). Another group was termed "non-physical," as they liked to read books, magazines, watch television, and play table games (e.g. cards, chess or bridge). Other activities included visiting amusement parks, theme parks, attending spectator sporting events, visiting friends and relatives, taking cruises, visiting casinos, and spiritual or religious activities.

According to their responses, this group of retirees undertook these various vacation activities for five fundamental reasons. The first of these was "excitement," covering such benefits as enjoying developing skills, engaging in a contest, having the opportunity for self-expression and growing as a person. A second major form of benefit was "social bonding." This included taking pleasure in helping other people, feeling that they belonged, and strengthening existing relationships. The third main motivation was "meeting role expectations," made up of things like duties that were expected of them by their families, or by their friends. Another major motivation was "relaxation," including having a restful experience, doing things that promoted health and wellbeing, and generally feeling relaxed.

Further analysis of the survey's findings by the researchers suggested that there were basically four types of traveler in terms of their destination activities: "learner," "urban," "entertained," and "spiritual." A third of the sample fell into the learner category, being most interested in the educational activities. However, the largest group was the urban sample, which included nearly half of the respondents. Their replies clustered around the city-based activities. A third group was made up of only about 12 percent of participants and their primary interest was in being entertained (for example, they scored highest on the physical and simple pleasure activities, and lowest on the educational and spiritual factors). Finally, about 6 percent of the sample scored extremely high on the spiritual items and very low on the city-based activities. In summary, these findings suggest some interesting patterns, ones that have been found in other surveys.[17] However, the authors speculated that some factors, such as "excitement," are particularly significant in a group of retired people (because the excitement and challenge associated with work is no longer available). In particular, the sub-sample labeled "spiritual" represents a distinct characteristic of the retired sample (i.e. this has not been found in previous surveys of the general population).

Another interesting association was the surprising lack of difference in the reason for the highly varied activities. While the "learners" experienced significantly more excitement than those in the "urban" group, and the "entertained" group experienced more relaxation than the other groups, there were very few other differences. This suggests that, despite differences in the particular activities that retired people engage in while traveling, they reported very similar psychological benefits. This is consistent with the idea that successful aging involves making the most of what is available within the particular travel activities, enabling travelers to learn more about the world and more about themselves.

Prior research has suggested a number of additional motives for travelling as part of retirement: escaping from a mundane environment, creativity, nostalgia, visiting friends and relatives, revitalizing, and memorable moments. Interestingly, these reasons seem to apply to us all, regardless of age, socioeconomic status, or the type of holiday. All-in-all, it appears that travelling and vacations definitely promote wellbeing, although briefly (research suggests that the benefits are lost within a month).[18]

However, as we all know, travelling is not always straightforward. Studies have identified numerous constraints: social isolation, the perceived safety of a destination, worry about the health care resources at travel destinations, concerns about a lack of foreign language skills (and the anticipated difficulties in communication), feeling uneasy being away from home, or simply lacking the physical ability to cope with the demands of travel. These constraints need to be weighed against the benefits.

In a Taiwanese study, these constraints and motives were combined to try to establish the overall picture.[19] This indicated that age, income, employment status, relaxation, novelty, socialization, and personal constraints were the main factors affecting retired people travelling overseas. In other words, the travel that retired people undertake is not simply determined by one or two factors such as the availability of money, but rather by a complex mixture of material and psychological factors.

Another influence is the curious business of being ill on holiday, or "leisure sickness." Based on a survey of over 1,000 people in the Netherlands,[20] it appears that 3 to 4 percent report more illness on holidays (and at weekends) than when at work. This is often our seasonal bout of the flu, but there are also examples of more frequent heart attacks. The reason is not known, though contenders include the stressors associated with travelling (traffic congestion, irritating fellow travelers, etc.); and marked changes in exercise, eating, and drinking. Intriguingly, those who are especially dedicated to their work, who seek perfection, and who find it hard to relax seem to be most at risk. Medical advice encourages a gradual approach: have a few days at home before setting off (there is also evidence that holidays of about a week provide the greatest pleasure).[21]

## Religion and Spirituality

We have just seen that there can be a religious dimension to travelling, and indeed religion represents a major influence running through the lives of many, providing them with a profound source of support. By "religion," I refer to agreed beliefs and behaviors about spiritual reality, God, morality, purpose; and the communication of these in socially distinctive, formalized ways, epitomized in church services. In a study of religion in the lives of a sample of nearly 300 recently-bereaved Americans aged 50 plus, the best outcomes were reported by those who drew upon their religious beliefs in order to find meaning and rebuild their worlds.[22] Research indicates that religion is usually associated with health, both indirectly (through social capital) and directly (through the consoling effect of religious beliefs about death). This latter effect is thought to arise in part from the way that religion encourages adaptation and healthy living. For example, Seventh Day Adventists believe that remaining healthy is a religious obligation, so they are vegetarians, teetotal, and non-smokers. Believers make up about half the population of America's healthiest city, Loma Linda. After all, the seven deadly sins of Christianity include gluttony (over-eating), anger, and sloth (avoiding work and exercise), not to mention traits that you will not find within "positive psychology" (i.e. greed, envy, and pride). Christians are encouraged to develop virtues to combat these sins, such as abstinence, patience, cooperation, and diligence. Other major religions do likewise, generally advocating temperance, self-regulation, and compassion. At their core these virtues can be seen as promoting faith and direction to peoples' lives and also wisdom in travelling that path. This wisdom includes studying scriptures and meditational practices that develop self-awareness, thoughtfulness (e.g. considering different perspectives), a keen sense of social justice, and collective discipline.

While religion can be viewed as a major support for retirees, in the interests of balance one should also note that terrible things are done in the name of religion, as in provoking hatred, injustice, intolerance, and the modern horrors of terrorism. This perspective is addressed by Richard Dawkins in *The God Delusion*,[23] in which he presented a belief in God as irrational and religion as having a corrupting influence on values and ethics, as illustrated by social evils perpetuated throughout history. Similarly, for some psychologists religious life raises questions about mental health, in that the supernatural belief systems (e.g. voices, visions, and possession by the devil) and the solemn practicing of rituals (akin to obsessive-compulsive disorder) can be suggestive of what Freud considered a *collective neurosis*, a maladaptive illusion. However, research indicates little connection between religion and mental health problems (e.g. the voices and visions in religious experience are pleasant, sought-after and controllable, unlike the related mental health problems). However, in general therapists are increasingly interested in aspects of religious experience, as in the popularity of Buddhism's "mindfulness meditation" as a treatment for depression; and therapists share a commitment to fostering wellbeing and supporting people in trying to make the most of their lives.

In summary, religion can be regarded as a powerful tool, capable of doing good or harm, depending on its interpretation in everyday life. A popular alternative is spirituality, which also fosters wellbeing. It can be contrasted with religion in being a more individualized and private interest (e.g. concerning one's place in the universe), in being more emotionally-focused (aimed at developing a richer, more authentic inner life), and being more directed at achieving one's potential ("self-actualization" or personal transformation). In a survey reported in 2009,[24] 40 percent of Americans described themselves as pursuing the option of "spiritual but not religious." Another option is to separate the formal beliefs of religion from their practices. As Alain De Botton outlined in *Religion for Atheists*,[25] atheists and agnostics should consider *stealing* some of the good practices from religion:

> One can be left cold by the doctrines of the Christian Trinity and the Buddhist Eightfold Path and yet at the same time be interested in the ways in which religions ... promote morality, engender a spirit of community, make use of art and architecture, inspire travels, train minds and encourage gratitude at the beauty of Spring.[26]

He recognized that religions confer two general benefits: encouraging us to live together in harmony, and helping us to cope. For believers, religion can confer other specific benefits, such as providing a profound source of hope and direction in all areas of life.

## Conclusions

Thankfully, there are many supportive arrangements that can aid your retirement transition, from appreciating your more general "High Street" social supporters to feeling embedded in your culture and community. These supportive layers can nurture and guide us through retirement, whether based on an allotment, travelling, a club or a social group (e.g. The University of the Third Age: U3A). For many, religion is a profound source of comfort and support, and it was noted that atheists can also benefit from some of the behaviors promoted.

# 6

# Learning from Life

*The road to wisdom?*
*Well, it's plain & simple to express:*
*Err and err and err again,*
*But less and less and less.*[1]

One of our especially impressive characteristics is adaptability. By and large, we deal effectively with what life throws at us, whether this is coping with everyday challenges or making significant transitions that can mean re-inventing ourselves. If you are reading this in your retirement, pause for a moment to marvel at how many obstacles you have overcome to get this far, and reflect on how you have developed over the years. We have made such progress by adapting, mostly due to our extraordinary capacity for learning. To quote one author, we are "the learning species,"[2] in that our distinctive specialization, in comparison to other species, is learning itself. Learning can be defined as the lasting changes we make as a result of experience, most obviously how we develop in the specialized environments we create to foster learning, such as schools and universities. Learning also permeates our everyday activity, being a process of dealing with practical issues through trial and error, with the result that we acquire knowledge, skills, or attitudes that equip us better to cope throughout our lifespan. Clearly, this process is of huge importance to coping with retirement, which is why this chapter is devoted to learning.

In particular, this chapter focuses on learning from everyday experience ("experiential learning"), treating it as the foundation for a process of adjustment and fulfillment. According to current psychological theory, this

*The Psychology of Retirement: Coping with the Transition from Work*, First Edition. By D. Milne.
© 2013 D. Milne. Published 2013 by John Wiley & Sons, Ltd.

foundation is inherent from before birth. Old theories assumed that, until mature, an infant saw the world as a "booming, buzzing confusion." Current thinking builds on the realization that infants start to learn in the womb, emerging into the public world already primed to attend to certain sounds and movements. Thereafter development continues, with earlier learning forming the basis for things like the automatic assumptions we make about our world. In this sense, we learn repeatedly and progressively, building on what we already know. This means that the way we learn from our experience is like a long and winding trail up the mountain that is our life: sometimes we will get lost and find ourselves back where we started, but such mistakes help us to deepen our understanding of where we went wrong. Of course, like a mountain path, the journey is not straightforward – just as the trail undulates so we do not always develop smoothly. I will concentrate on how to avoid the metaphorical rock-falls and steep ravines along the way.

I intend to focus on specific thoughts, feelings and behaviors that affect our journey along this trail, to highlight the things that aid our development. I want to answer the question: what does it take to profit from our experience? I will be examining reflection, a prized example of rational thinking, together with the other main phases of experiential learning (i.e. understanding, planning, doing, and feeling). I will also consider the immediate and longer-term consequences of this learning process, such as the way that reflection can promote personal insights; or how a better understanding can aid us in making sound decisions. The argument I will be advancing is that attention to each of these phases of learning can equip us better to cope, giving us a better chance of turning our retirement transition into a positive experience. As usual, I will give attention to some of the typical challenges that retirement brings, such as dealing with anxieties (e.g. about death), coming to terms with our regrets, and developing expertise. To address these challenges I will emphasize resourceful strategies, like drawing on the "self-help" literature, plus useful parallels between everyday social support and therapy. Therefore, in terms of this book's RECIPE for coping, this chapter is mostly concerned with the role played by *intellectual activity*.

## Reflection

Most of us will reflect several times a day, and when significant events arise we may spend days reflecting on them. In the case study below, we find Ben reflecting on whether to retire or not:

**Figure 6.1** Retirement can feel like taking the plunge into scary waters

"it's like standing on the edge of the pool: shall I jump? But you have to realize that you can swim, be brave, stay positive about the decision and go with it [see Figure 6.1]. You need to trust yourself and remain positive. It might not be the right decision ultimately, but you have to believe that it was the correct decision at the time."

Unlike day-dreaming and other forms of thinking about events, reflection is defined as an active and persistent process of thinking so as to decide what we should believe or do. It may be about something that has happened in our lives, or about the future; and it may be triggered by something perplexing, something that surprised you, or about a challenge that you face. It is often uncomfortable, as:

> Reflective thinking is always more or less troublesome because it involves overcoming the inertia that inclines one to accept suggestions at their face value; it involves willingness to endure a condition of mental unrest and disturbance.[3]

Given, as John Dewey suggests, reflective thinking is troublesome, how can we reflect most effectively?

- Allocate some "quality" time (e.g. no distractions).
- Try to recapture or create the key experience or issue that you want to reflect on as vividly as possible.
- Attend to any feelings that may arise (see the "feeling" section below on how you might deal with these).
- Review what happened or consider a future concern to gain perspective (addressing relevant questions can be a great help, as outlined shortly).
- For things that have already happened, decide on any lessons that are worth learning. This might be achieved by linking it your prior experience (e.g. is this something that keeps on happening – identify whether it might be a pattern or "lifetrap"). Or it might be that you can benefit from the reflection, by combining this with related ideas to strengthen your understanding (like Ben, above). Or you may want to apply the understanding in order to address a problem, or to test it out (to decide whether it was sound or not).

As mentioned, questions are a prime way to enable reflection. For instance, asking yourself: "what do I already know about this?"; "have I overcome problems like this before?" and "what's this like?" can help to access knowledge that you barely realized you possessed. Because "all learning is re-learning," there will almost certainly be something that you can draw on to answer such questions, if you are patient and thoughtful. *The Book of Answers*[4] is rich in stimulating questions of this kind. Some examples I generated are: "what makes now a good time to act?"; "which actions might improve things?"; "what do you need to attend to right now?"; "how might you explore the issue, with playful curiosity?"; "what's your biggest doubt?"; "what makes it better to wait?" and "what's the thing you are probably going to have to accept?"

As a result of successful reflection, we can achieve a number of useful outcomes: heightened self-awareness (e.g. recognizing those recurring patterns); consolidation of your beliefs (just like Ben); clarification of things (e.g. how they differ, or are the same); understanding (analyzing problems down to their elements); transfer (extrapolating your reflections to other situations); and evaluation (judging the worth or accuracy of a reflection). These benefits of reflection underline why it is so highly rated as a way of learning and adapting.

## Regrets

Reflection can make you aware of your regrets: the emotionally-painful business of realizing that you might have handled things more effectively at some critical point in your past. This is often a significant regret, perhaps a marriage that failed, or maybe it concerns not pursuing a particular promotion or career. Regrets also relate to everyday issues (e.g. regretting eating or drinking too much last night). Surveys conducted in the US rank regrets about career and education as the most common (i.e. disappointment over what we have achieved: e.g. not studying harder towards qualifications), closely followed by romantic regrets (e.g. "lost loves").[5] Other major themes were personal shortcomings and status.

In terms of coping, regrets can encourage corrective thinking, particularly if there is still some means to reverse the regret. However, if there is no way back, then coping often focuses on reframing, suppressing, or diminishing the regret. In terms of reframing (see Chapter 3), we may feel bad about something that went wrong, but recognize that we learnt an important lesson. Suppressing refers to avoidance of the regret, by distraction or by superimposing an alternative thought (e.g. re-focusing on an imminent challenge). Similarly, we can transform a regret by devaluing its importance, or by elaborating and strengthening the justification for the regretted action. In such ways, we can cope with our regrets and work towards some kind of closure and respite.

When the regret is concerning taking no action in a given situation or event, then as a rule this appears to be easier to handle than having behaved in some decisive way, though the passage of time and the severity of the regret play a role in how well we cope. Over time, it seems that for most people regrets about not acting persist the longest; and that the more severe or pronounced the regret the longer it will feature in our reflections. Of course, these are sweeping generalizations and individuals will differ significantly in the extent and nature of their reflections on regrets. One telephone survey asked participants (370 adult Americans) to describe a significant regret.[6] It was found that women had significantly more romantic regrets, which the authors attributed to their greater valuation of social relationships. Men were more inclined to identify work-related regrets, particularly those concerning their limited education. Older adults in the same study were notable because, although they had less time or energy to repair regrets, this was compensated for because they were said to "possess superior powers of positive reappraisal, to balance out the picture."[7] The researchers considered the findings highlighted the core need to belong: "People crave strong, stable relationships and are unhappy when they lack them; regret embodies this principle."[8] They concluded that regrets can act as a stimulus to constructive reflection, helping us to develop.

## Understanding

Reflection on things like regrets is a private act, drawing on our personal knowledge. To reflect effectively, this should be supplemented by public knowledge, such as the known facts about an issue (e.g. illness symptoms and statistics), and ideas for coping (e.g. what experts say, or treatment guidelines drawn from research). Combined with reflection, this public understanding of issues allows us to understand better the matter at hand. This is one of the reasons why research findings are included in this book. Another example is what we can learn from books: the literature is rich in ideas for understanding retirement and how to cope with it, especially "self-help" books: *Manage Your Mind: The Mental Fitness Guide,* written by psychologist Gillian Butler and psychiatrist Tony Hope in 2007 is one such example.[9] This book is not specific to retirement, but is intended to help people cope with the general stresses and strains of life, drawing on a scientific, cognitive-behavior therapy (CBT) approach. This is a best-selling guide that covers a range of vital dimensions of successful functioning, including advice on building self-confidence, overcoming depression, establishing and maintaining successful relationships, and developing your potential. To summarize the advice given in the book: we all have difficulties that need attention. Facing up to difficulties is part of a problem-solving cycle: step one is to identify the problem as clearly and precisely as possible (specifying how frequently it occurs, how discomforting it feels, and how long it has been going on); step two is to generate as many possible solutions as possible, ideally adopting an imaginative mentality in the early stages, to maximize fresh thinking. The next step is to select the most promising of these solutions and try to implement it, adopting an experimental approach. The final step is to evaluate whether or not the solution is effective. Revisions may well be necessary before a successful solution is found. Other helpful advice in this book is not to waste time on problems that cannot be solved, but instead to re-focus on achievable results, tackling one problem at a time; and to focus on changing oneself, rather than trying to change other people.

One of the most difficult topics to truly grasp is our mortality. After all, we spend most of our lives believing deep down (i.e. at an emotional or unconscious level) that we are indestructible, even though rationally we know we only have a finite life: "Everybody knows they're going to die, but no one really believes it."[10] Such self-deception can include some black humor, to make the topic more bearable: "It's not that I'm afraid to die, I just don't want to be there when it happens."[11] This self-deception is maintained by a kind of magical thinking, which allows us to go on believing in our fantasy of immortality, only occasionally disrupted by unwelcome experiences of loss, separation, or illness. Some say that it is only when both our parents are dead that we truly acknowledge our mortality. If pushed on the topic, we may say that we "take one day at a time," express fatalistic views (e.g. "whatever will be, will be"), or ascribe responsibility to others ("fate is in the hands of God"). Even when we realize that death awaits us, we tend to brush such thoughts aside, avoiding the attendant feelings. Or we may hold comforting spiritual or religious beliefs, ones that offer eternal life through reincarnation, a place in heaven, or enlightenment. From a purely psychological perspective, such beliefs make sense as a way of reducing our anxieties about death.

Such is our anxiety that in some communities death is a taboo topic, while in others it is discussed as little as possible. In one study of people aged over 75 years, conducted in Baltimore,[12] 19 of the 20 people interviewed were reluctant to think about, discuss, or plan for future illnesses. As a result of this denial, most had not made a Will. The authors concluded that these people "were resistant to planning in advance for the hypothetical future, particularly for serious illness when death is possible."[13] My view is that the best way to cope effectively with this much-avoided topic is to face up to it. I think we can feel more comfortable about it, moving on to more immediate matters without it distracting us. There is also a more positive reason for considering our eventual death, which is to focus our minds on what we want to achieve while still alive and kicking. Therapists Robert Firestone and Joyce Catlett have led groups for many people in the US. They noted that: "Ironically, the awareness and acceptance of one's mortality, combined with learning to express one's sadness, anger, and death fears, can lead to ... deeper satisfaction, more personal freedom, and a greater appreciation for the gift of life."[14]

Death is surprisingly difficult to define, including the difference between "clinical" and "legal" death (the latter is based on brain death), and the fact that we can have been clinically dead (i.e. ceased breathing and have our heart stopped) yet resume living, due to modern resuscitation techniques or technology (e.g. defibrillator, life support systems). The definition of death is: "the permanent termination of the biological functions necessary to sustain life." In developing countries death is more often due to infectious diseases, primarily TB, malaria, and AIDS. In the Western world death is mainly a result of heart disease, strokes, or cancer. Old age leads to death due to a progressive weakening of our bodies, as cells and systems start to dysfunction. Part of this growing imbalance is thought to be due to our genes, which are decreasingly invested in our survival, as we move away from reproduction. A technical term for this is "entropy," being the tendency of any system to move from order and efficiency to disorder and dysfunction, heralding a loss of vital energy and a reduced capacity for change.

The experience of death is perhaps what we fear most, particularly the possibility of extreme pain, but of course we struggle to know what to expect. Near-death experiences are thought by some to provide a clue, as when those who have been resuscitated recount their experience (in a Gallup poll, some 8 million Americans reported experiencing near-death). The consensus from such reports is that there is a mental/spiritual detachment from the body, followed by feelings of painlessness, levitation (looking down on our body, perhaps seeing resuscitation being administered, then extreme fear or total serenity, e.g. a sense of security or warmth), and finally the presence of a bright light. Such reports go back at least as far as Plato's Republic, where the mythical soldier also described experiencing the after-life and reincarnation. Paranormal specialists tend to view this consensus as "proof" of an afterlife, whereas medical specialists suggest that these experiences are consistent with hallucinations and the physical effects of reduced oxygen levels in the brain.

From a psychological perspective, fear of dying is strong for the majority of the population, and remains marked throughout their lifespan.

Surprisingly, according to one survey, the fear consistently decreases on admission to a hospice. When this fear becomes exaggerated, irrational and interferes with one's life then the term "thanataphobia" might be appropriate (from "thanatos," the Greek for death). In sufferers, this phobia often appears to be linked to religious devotion, perhaps linked to terrifying messages about eternal damnation or punishment, explicitly linked to failing to stick to the path of righteousness. On the other hand, religion affords a very comforting message about overcoming death through a positive transition to everlasting life.

For us all, the fear is also about facing the unknown, about loss of control (mental and physical deterioration), or fear of severe pain, or loss of dignity, Many fear for the consequences of our death for our family (e.g. that they will suffer emotionally, financially or socially), or the fear of simply non-existence (nothingness, of being totally alone in a void). Like any fear, these perceptions can be adaptive, encouraging us to take due care to postpone death by maintaining health and wellbeing. Some of the methods outlined in this book may be helpful, such as thinking rationally and using meditation. However, there are stages that seem to be fairly common when considering our eventual death, points at which we might benefit from the use of psychological methods. These stages are seen as part of a journey involving recognition that death is approaching, withdrawal, separation from family and friends, and revisiting memories of our life ("life review"). *On Death and Dying*[15] outlines five stages of coping with death: denial, anger, bargaining, depression, and ultimately acceptance. It should be said that this was never intended to be anything more than a framework for understanding what might be happening during the dying process, rather than some kind of fixed sequence. In terms of the acceptance phase, it has helpfully been suggested that we should address five tasks:

1. Asking for forgiveness (for the hurts we have caused, the unfulfilled dreams: cleansing the psychological wounds).
2. Offering forgiveness (in turn, showing loving by excusing or accepting wrongs done against you, including things that have caused shame).
3. Offering heartfelt thanks (expressing gratitude for your life).
4. Convey sentiments of love (let your loved one's know that you love them; this can be simply said or written, yet surprisingly powerful. Acts of caring can serve where finding the words to say is difficult, such as touching, grooming, or massaging).
5. Say "goodbye" (a vital concluding message that appears to have motivated many to hold onto life long enough to utter this word).

So, we have just coped appropriately by facing up to some of the realities of that "grim reaper in the shadows!" There is undoubtedly a huge degree of uncertainty and anxiety surrounding death and dying, but I believe that we do ourselves proud when we encounter this reality by coping as effectively as possible, by drawing appropriately on social support, by discussing death and the associated anxieties with others, by using an awareness of death to heighten our appreciation for life. Paradoxically, when we inhibit thoughts of our death, we can "deaden" our lives, numbing anxious feelings through isolating activities and by distancing ourselves from our loved ones, perhaps by developing a hypercritical attitude to ourselves, self-denial, and the use of substances or fixed routines to control our feelings. By contrast, while a greater acceptance of death carries with it sadness and anxiety, it also tends to foster: spontaneity in our social involvement; a realization that time is limited; flexible and genuine personal functioning; and deeper self-acceptance.

## Planning

According to the theory of "experiential learning,"[16] to cope optimally with stressors and our transition we should channel our thinking into clear retirement plans, featuring specific, achievable goals particularly incorporating financial planning, something which the media indicate is fast becoming a dwindling activity (as people concentrate on staying afloat in the present, given "the credit crunch," the "failed banks," frozen salaries, disappointing pension products, and other threats). For some the plan may nothing more than trusting that their savings or pension will suffice. Others may focus by altering their circumstances, perhaps downsizing their material resources (e.g. car, home), developing a more frugal approach to expenditure, or by resuming work. Alternatively, some may focus on gaining more state benefit, or rely on luck (such as winning the lottery) or depend on an inheritance. Our case study reflects this thinking when Ben and Katie:

> spontaneously mentioned a concern about a financial aspect of their retirement regarding their daughter: they had "been supporting her with a weekly allowance" which was "soon to stop, with her getting a job." There is clearly a concern that the financial situation may become harsher as time passes, which they fear may impinge on their lifestyle.

Of course, many services are on offer to aid financial planning, from personal finance advisors who can assist with investments and other products (e.g.

life insurance policies), to banks and other institutions which may help by lending money. Advisory leaflets are available through various voluntary and state-run organizations (e.g. in the UK there is the government-run Pension Advisory Service and a Pension Forecasting Team). Advice is also readily available on managing debts, tax credits, and benefits.

Calculating how much income you may have from any pension is in many ways the easiest part of the planning equation. It should be fairly clear how much income you can expect from your pension scheme, and a financial advisor will be able to provide you with a range of possible incomes for any funds you are able to invest (e.g. your retirement "lump sum"). The more difficult part of the equation is trying to forecast how much you will need, as this is based on your personal sense of how much it will take to give you peace of mind in an uncertain future. While there are "pension calculator" systems which can provide an objective answer (and experts estimate that we need between 60–80 percent of our final annual salary to manage in retirement), there are inherent unknowns, as indicated by the credit crunch. This is not to question the value of facts and figures, and one sensible coping strategy is to purchase a "year planner" and predict what your expenses will be, in detail, over a hypothetical retirement year. Will there be a holiday? What about special occasions, or presents? Would you expect to visit friends abroad, or to drive extensively in support of your children (e.g. acting as a grandparent)? Do you want to add a contingency fund, and would that put your mind at rest?

Even with a carefully considered financial plan, there remain uncertainties. You don't know how long your retirement will last, whether you will need domestic support, residential care, or other kinds of personal help (and whether you will be content with what the state provides). You may unexpectedly become a carer, with significant effects on your life (possibly including spending far less than you had planned). In addition, although it is wise to look ahead, trying to imagine how life will be in retirement is difficult. If you are going from full-time work to no work it will be tricky to anticipate how you will spend your time and therefore how much money you will need. Also, there may be a void where once there was work, and filling that may involve unforeseen costs (e.g. an expensive new hobby). Even if you have firm ideas how you would like to use your time in retirement (e.g. spending unrestricted hours at a hobby that previously you did at weekends), in the reality of retirement, these expectations may simply not work (as in the case study in Chapter 2). You may have to find new ways of spending your time, bringing unexpected expense. Another possibility, one that affects many retirees, is that you may feel that you want to travel, which can vary hugely in cost. Last, even if your predictions about your money needs are sound, you may unexpectedly feel the need to resume work (part-time or occasionally), as you experience a need for the structure, role (status) and identity that it provided. These unknowns will all influence the equation that addresses the difficult question of "how much do I need?" One way to cope is to ask yourself how you would feel if "plan A" fell apart – do you think you could cope with a more frugal lifestyle? Or can you see yourself coming up with "plan B"? If you feel reasonably relaxed about managing on less, then this reduces the pressure.

In conclusion, one of the most difficult aspects of planning is uncertainty about the future, which is compounded by highly subjective issues, including our changing personal needs and social circumstances, and our confidence about coping with uncertainty (including our capacity to generate finances through part-time working). In this sense, retirement can perhaps best be seen as an expedition. To plan for this, we will need maps and guides (financial advisors, pension calculators, this book), advice from others (friends and relatives who have already retired), supplies (food, heat, money), a base camp (housing), transport, support from others (relatives, neighbors), and ways to communicate with them.

## Doing

Modern psychological theory also indicates the benefits that come from taking an active role in our own learning. In contrast to how we sometimes learn in a fairly passive way (e.g. leisurely observing how others cope with varying stressors), we learn more effectively when we consciously address issues, especially when we realize how we have resolved an issue. This is because when we are actively involved we are more explicit about what we understand, more systematic about testing this, and more likely to transfer our improved awareness to new problems or situations. This ability, to be aware of our own thinking, is called "meta-cognition." We sometimes become aware of it in the form of an internal, private "conversation" with ourselves, an ability that is a sophisticated way of using thinking (e.g. reflection) to guide our actions. Expertise is the capacity to rapidly spot key features or patterns so as to realize the significance of the situation and to draw on a deep understanding in order to have several options for addressing a difficulty; to consider these options; and to then act fluently and decisively. This has been studied with chess players, where the chess masters were shown to be better at recognizing the pattern of pieces on the board of an incomplete game, and had a better understanding of what was at stake and the best moves to take, compared to novices. The same elements of expertise are identifiable in everyday situations, such as when a qualified person tackles a problem that you have been working on as a layperson. For example:

- A tradesman analyses a problem with your central heating system, quickly realizing how certain "clues" point to the reason for the fault.
- A mechanic quizzes you for two to three key bits of information, before plunging under the car bonnet to pinpoint the faulty component.
- A sports coach points out that, if you keep hitting the ball as you are doing right now, you will end up with a specific injury.
- Also doctors, dentists, and others, who use more obvious forms of expertise.

This is one way of understanding the popular expression that one has learned through "the university of life" or "the school of hard knocks." Our skills in meta-cognition benefit from our becoming more aware of how we are thinking (i.e. listening to our internal conversations); from drawing out the main ideas or concepts that we are using (i.e. ideas that help to organize our thinking); and from drawing on many relevant examples, so we understand things in depth (for more on this, see and Bransford *et al.*'s *How People Learn* and other Recommended Reading).

Research indicates that there are several critical actions that foster our wellbeing. These revolve around facing up to our fears, so that we learn that the things we are anxious about are actually not that bad. Methods include demonstrating that nothing terrible happens ("reality testing"), practicing new coping skills, tackling things gradually, and building on small successes. In relation to dealing with situations involving loss, such as bereavement, there is reason to believe that physical activity, hobbies, volunteering, leisure activities, and general socializing provide an important source of restoration and some respite from the dominant feeling of grief. There is also a need to attend to the everyday "activities of daily living," the necessary self-care and safety-promoting activities that are often secondary to loss and grieving. Of course, many of these actions can also be beneficial in coping with retirement generally. As Placido Domingo put it: "If I rest, I rust."[17] This is illustrated in the case study, where both Katie and Ben were keeping themselves busy and purposeful. In particular: Ben has been undertaking voluntary work with the Samaritans and has almost completed his training course.

## Feeling

One of the difficult challenges during retirement is dealing with some of the accompanying emotions, which can be many. For instance, there's a poignant feeling which can accompany the loss of sexual prowess. Jack Nicholson, renowned as one of Hollywood's great seducers, was interviewed by *The Mail on Sunday* at the age of 73. He said that those days were over: "I've struck bio-gravity ... I can't hit on women in public any more. I didn't decide this; it just doesn't feel right ... that makes me sad ... but I also think that a lot of improvements in my character have come through ageing and the diminishing of powers."[18] Similarly, former Member of Parliament Tony Benn said: "Ageing is a form of liberation. You become a Buddhist by default because you rid yourself of all kinds of desire."[19] Others have noted positive feelings, as in the relief of escaping into retirement from vexatious work, or the satisfaction that comes from finally having time for a hobby or interest.

There are also negative feelings, such as those associated with the loss of a partner. To demonstrate the force of emotions, this has been described as:

> profound sadness, pining, depression, altered identity, negative health outcomes, loneliness and the withdrawal of support networks. Additionally, there is evidence of considerable stress associated with the role changes that accompany widowhood, particularly those due to disruptions in life patterns and daily routine, taking on new unfamiliar tasks, and changes in social activities and relationships.[20]

Then there are perhaps the strangest feelings of them all – the surprising *absence* of feelings when everything tells us to expect them. In clinical terms this is called "dissociation," the compartmentalizing of thoughts, behaviors and feelings that are normally integrated. In everyday language, it is as if we put on some mental armor to protect us from facing up to some awful feeling. In surveys of the UK population, examples have been reported by some 60 percent of respondents.[21] These include feeling detached or cocooned, being lost in thought, or of operating on "autopilot" during a situation where extreme emotions would be expected (or of being unable to recall much of what happened during a difficult situation). It can therefore be a kind of selective amnesia, where afterwards we can see that this actually helped us to keep functioning (e.g. dealing with an emergency). In this sense, dissociation is the unconscious psychological equivalent of taking psychoactive drugs or alcohol to cope with intolerable feelings. People in this state appear emotionally detached or feel numbed, and are preoccupied or distracted: there is something unspoken keeping them "out of reach" and "shut off" from reality, though self-awareness of this state is also typically lacking, as if we have returned to the protection and safety of the womb.

Major examples of dissociation can be striking and so often make the news, as in someone's temporary loss of identity or change in personality placing them in an unusual situation. People have been known to embark on an unplanned trip or to simply wander off in a detached state, even starting a new life somewhere, where they are blissfully unaware of their former lives. This may only become clear when the individual "re-awakens" or regains awareness, usually feeling unsettled and distressed. More extreme instances include "multiple personality disorder" and "depersonalization." It appears that earlier experiences of trauma (e.g. combat, life-threatening accidents, assault) make people vulnerable to more extreme reactions. These can be understood as unconscious or automatic psychological responses, an in-built defense mechanism that allows us to escape from intolerable, unmanageable situations. Although this affords short-term respite, the long-term consequences can be severe, including poor adjustment and general dysfunction (e.g. anxiety, low self-esteem, substance abuse).

It is, therefore, possible to see a spectrum of emotional reactions related to retirement, from elation to depression, with all manner of "shades of grey" in between. In this chapter the focus is on how we can work with such emotions in ways that help us to learn and grow. This includes trying to recognize and understand these feelings, a kind of emotional processing, so that we more readily accept and learn from our feelings. Therapists believe that unpleasant feelings of the kind that accompany accidents and traumas (e.g. recurring nightmares, panic attacks, or intrusive thoughts) need to be "worked through," rather than ignored or avoided. An example is the process of "assimilation," where a therapist will encourage a client to describe a problematic experience, bringing it into full consciousness. When fully felt, this will tend to trigger some unpleasant memories and feelings of anxiety. The client will naturally want to stop attending to the memory, "warding-off" unwelcome images and unwanted thoughts in order to end the anxiety. At this stage there may only be a vague awareness of the nature of the problem, so the therapist may work on further clarifying what it means, drawing out details and related feelings in order to try and grasp why it is so upsetting, and to then consider ways of reframing what happened or the feeling reaction. In this way some insight into the problem may emerge, with a gradual reduction in the anxiety, so we can gradually "assimilate" unpleasant events, as if digesting them (i.e. making them an acceptable part of who we are). This is a corrective emotional experience, one of the main methods that allow us to come to terms with unpleasant feelings, at least enough to enable us to function more freely and effectively.

Note that there are several key ingredients in this assimilation process between therapist and client: focused attention; exploration of why something is so distressing for that individual (its personal meaning or significance); awareness-raising; defining and labeling what is upsetting and what we are feeling; a release of tension, culminating in more rational thinking and insight (a deeper understanding). Note too that the therapist will normally be highly supportive of the client, creating a collaborative relationship based on warmth, respect, empathy, acceptance, trust, and genuineness. This therapeutic alliance helps the client to face up to unpleasant material and endure dealing with it long enough to work through it (e.g. by getting things out in the open, giving a sense of catharsis).

These examples are of the more extreme feeling reactions, which may be helpful in placing your own feelings in perspective. Some of the methods described could be useful in less severe reactions, as could the support of someone in whom we feel we can confide. The case study that follows is rich in examples of mutual support.

## Case Study: Ben and Katie – Different Experiences of Retiring

Ben retired a couple of years ago at the age of 57, following 40 years working in the same factory. Katie followed, retiring at the age of 55, also having worked in the same factory for a long time – 39 years. Ben was Katie's boss for the last few years of his working life. As they put it, Ben was the boss at work, Katie was the boss at home.

### Stressful Experience of Retiring

While Ben had planned his retirement for some time and "slipped into it, like a well-worn shoe ... seamless," Katie's retirement was a more emotional period. Not only had she lost Ben's support as her manager following his retirement, but the job had become increasingly stressful. Her post of

Production Planner required her to purchase the basic materials and deal with the company's customers. There was a new computer system, competitive colleagues, and increasing pressure from the company to maximize profits. As a result, she began to suffer physically and psychologically, developing severe headaches and a reduction of her confidence. Katie began to view her work negatively: she "didn't want to be there." As tends to happen when things begin to go wrong, Katie also began to experience some envy and resentment: while she was going through this difficult period at work, Ben was well clear of the stressors, retired and enjoying himself. She became "weary of it all ... had enough ... can't cope anymore ... leave or look for another job." Here, then, we can see that "vicious cycle" occurring, as described in Chapter 2.

### Appraisal

Katie and Ben had gone through the "empty nest" transition when their only child had left home to go to university. Indeed, our interview was taking place a couple of days before her graduation. Her leaving home had created "a big hole: they missed her terribly and worried about her, as she is asthmatic." However, she had done well, and they were clearly proud of her achievement: not only had she graduated successfully, but had been head-hunted by a local firm, based on her outstanding final-year project. They were also proud that their daughter had "grown up to be such a nice woman ... all our friends like her ... she is respectful and patient ... thought she'd be a teacher, but she's got her own path and she's got her own skills through the degree and now she's got a job. We encouraged her to do what's right for her and thought it selfish to miss her ... but it's a happy loss."

Thus, although clearly feeling the absence of their only child, Katie and Ben took a positive perspective, reframing the loss as a necessary and proper stage in their daughter's development, and also part of their own transition. At the time of our interview, the sense of the "empty nest" was easing, being replaced by these positive perceptions and by other diversions.

### Coping

When asked about their coping strategies in relation to this "empty nest" experience, Ben and Katie mentioned a number of other activities that they had started during early retirement. These seemed to serve as a distraction from the absence of their daughter. As far as Ben was concerned: "the first thing I did was buy a bike ... confident there" (Ben had never learnt to drive a car, and so relied on Katie for transport). He also took up walking ("love it ... free") and he has begun to write about his favorite musician, Bob Dylan, having recently had a couple of articles accepted for a magazine. He was working on a third article, the theme being parallels between Dylan's songs and his own life. In addition to remaining physically and mentally active, Ben also underlined an important lesson of retirement, the importance of retaining social links. In his case this involves continuing to act as Secretary and player for his previous employer's 5-a-side football team. Indeed, according to Katie, Ben is by nature a social "lynchpin," ensuring that links are maintained between people and "acting as a catalyst in groups ... a contact point for socials." This occurs to such an extent that he is still arranging school reunions! He feels strongly that bringing people together is important, and that the quality of one's relationships is a major contributor to a satisfactory retirement.

Conversely, on several occasions they spontaneously mentioned concern regarding the financial aspect of their retirement. With regard to their daughter they had: "been supporting him with a weekly allowance which was soon to stop, with her getting a job." However, there is clearly a feeling that the financial situation may become harsher as time passes, which they fear may impinge on their lifestyle.

Socially they are "very active anyway ... very busy doing nothing ... all sorts of things." For Katie a key objective has been to lose weight and to get fitter, while overcoming some niggling health concerns, and she feels that she is "making progress." Their ambition is to spend some time travelling the West coast of the US, to explore the area. However, as Katie is the sole driver, both of them feel a little daunted at the prospect, though Ben now proposes to start taking lessons. He is clearly somewhat ambivalent about driving, perhaps as neither of his own parents drove a car. According to Katie "deep down Ben doesn't want to drive." They are concerned about the logistics of this trip to the point that they have considered inviting their daughter along, partly so that she can assist with the driving.

Ben still has friends from his school days 50 years ago, indeed he has strong social contacts all over the UK. Katie has a network of friends from work and they have weekly lunches. Together they host dinner parties. In general they are keeping busy, partly as Ben has been undertaking voluntary work with the Samaritans and has almost completed his training course (now acting as Probationer listener). This involves some shift work. He values this voluntary work, which he feels serves a valuable purpose in assisting people.

Katie is currently "a lady that lunches," having a weekly meeting with an old friend, and they are busy making plans for various outings. Like her own mother, Katie is also an accomplished painter and decorator, with a strong interest in gardening. But in these early months of her retirement she is still happy simply "mooching around" the house and sleeping a great deal, having "felt weary" after that very stressful final period at work.

## Learning from Life

I questioned whether either of them felt that their coping skills were becoming particularly well-developed. They emphatically agreed that such things change as time passes, but the main qualitative difference that they recounted was how having more time had a hugely beneficial effect: it meant that they could be more relaxed, fostering a "virtuous cycle," as they got to know their friends better in an unpressured way, so being able to enjoy the conversation more, and even have that extra glass of wine.

On reflection, I suspect that the most significant change that has come with time is not that they have discovered some amazing new activity or some dramatically improved way of doing things, but rather that they have become more confident and sure of the things that do matter to them. They spontaneously realized what people should know about retirement to make the best of it. According to Katie, money is an issue and thankfully she felt that as you get older you spend less. But they both felt that there is "never enough money" at any stage in life. Katie felt strongly that they needed to keep fit, so that they could enjoy what they could afford. Ben's focus was on the issue of when to retire, in my opinion, a clear example of their strength of belief. He drew the analogy with swimming: "it's like standing on the edge of the pool: shall I jump? But you have to realize that you can swim, be brave, stay positive about the decision and go with it. You need to trust yourself and remain positive. It might not be the right decision ultimately but you have to believe that it was the correct decision at the time."

## Summary

Whereas Ben knew many months in advance that he was going to retire and proceeded very smoothly towards retirement, for Katie the experience of work became particularly stressful over the last couple of years, resulting in significant relief when the time arrived. Ben clearly keeps himself very busy and is "never bored." He recounted how his peers will "phone him up half-way through the day, to ask 'what are you doing today, Ben?'" He tells them how busy he is, which causes them surprise.

Although as a couple they are in the first few months of retirement, it is clear that they have a lot going for them. Although they have some concerns regarding their financial situation, they clearly have a very warm and mutually-supportive relationship. A further strength is that they are positive in their outlook, naturally and quickly reframing concerns (such as finances), resulting in them feeling optimistic and confident about what the future may hold. They also have made a successful transition, having coped with the "empty nest" syndrome. Strengthened by that success, and by the great job they have done in bringing up their daughter, they can surely look forward to a happy and successful retirement.

## Summary and Conclusion

We are the *learning species*, superbly equipped to profit from the experiences that life brings. In particular, we adapt and develop through our ability to reflect, to draw on books and other sources of understanding, to plan and to test out our grasp, and have a capacity to recognize and assimilate strong feelings. Each of these parts of experiential learning was illustrated with an example, such as reflecting on our regrets. In the case of understanding we considered the somber matter of death. Anxieties about our death may encourage us to avoid the subject, but it is one of life's paradoxes that in doing so we may fail to fully appreciate life itself. One of the special challenges of retirement is to gracefully "let go" of the aspects of our lives that cause us to avoid feelings associated with death (such as status, money, or physical fitness) and instead become more aware and accepting of death. This can have a surprisingly enlivening impact and refresh our perception of our lives, such as the beauty of nature or the deep significance of our loved ones. We also considered how assimilating unpleasant feelings can help us to "move on", how planning can assist us in coping with the financial side of retirement, and how testing our understanding can keep our thinking straight.

I conclude from these examples that retirement proceeds best when it is approached actively and thoughtfully, drawing on our extraordinary capacity to learn and adapt.

# 7

# Learning for Life

*Grow old along with me, the best is yet to be, the last of life for which the first was made.[1]*

This upbeat quote underlines the idea of human development as a meaningful progression, introduced in the last chapter with ideas like the experiential learning cycle and especially that "all learning is relearning." Having addressed some fairly somber issues in that chapter (e.g. regrets and dying), this chapter will take a cue from Browning and consider a number of cheery ways to enhance our development during retirement. I will now elaborate this emphasis on learning by considering the main ways that we can develop our mind and body in our "third age." In terms of the mind, brain researcher Marian Diamond[2] listed four established ways in which we can help our brains to be as effective as possible. These are not new ideas, but rather ideas for which there is growing scientific support. They are:

1. Balanced diet: what we feed the brain plays a significant role.
2. Exercise on a daily basis helps the brain as well as the body.
3. Challenging the brain: use it or lose it. It is easy to get bored, under-stimulated, and allow the brain to grow "flabby."
4. Dealing with novelty: the brain thrives on newness in the challenges we face, as in drawing on new ideas, new learning, and fresh activities.

Regarding the body, in this chapter I will also outline why exercise is so vital for our wellbeing, and investigate some fascinating ways to develop excellence. These ways are drawn from sport, yet apply to much that we do.

*The Psychology of Retirement: Coping with the Transition from Work*, First Edition. By D. Milne.
© 2013 D. Milne. Published 2013 by John Wiley & Sons, Ltd.

We should, however, be wary of creating a false division between mind and body, as per Marian Diamond's emphasis on exercise above: we are clearly a complex system, so it is unlikely that any activity is completely separate from others. For instance, later I will summarize a recent study that evaluated the benefits of Yoga. Although the study was for lower back pain, the authors stressed that Yoga treats the whole person (e.g. mental relaxation alongside physical stretching).[3]

## Mind Over Matter

### Diet

You will have long since grasped the importance of a balanced diet, but research continues to indicate the essential role played by a sound diet: high in fiber (e.g. wholegrain cereals); high proportions of beans (legumes); multicolored fruit and vegetables (the "rainbow" diet); some deep, cold, sea-water fish (e.g. salmon); and minimizing salt, sugar, red meat, saturated fats, and fried food (i.e. reducing excess calorie intake).

Remember, the key word is "balanced," as foods like fat are still required. Diamond highlighted the role played by diet on the nerve cells, which have a white, fatty covering on their ends to speed up the conduction of electrical impulses from one nerve to another. There is research to suggest that children nowadays are showing a reduction in myelin, a clinical finding attributed to society's current emphasis on fat-free diets. Another important dietary ingredient is protein, which provides the material to develop and maintain nerve cells. Indeed, it seems that some cultures are aware of the relationship between protein and brain size. For example, in Kenya there appears to be a tradition where pregnant women deliberately avoid eating protein, because it means delivering a smaller baby. This led Diamond to conduct some laboratory experiments with rats, reducing their protein diets. As she feared, the brains suffered as a result of protein deprivation (the dendrites in baby rats whose mothers had reduced protein did not develop fully). Not only was there an initial deficit but this was not corrected by subsequently placing those protein-deprived babies in enriched living conditions (i.e. with lots of objects to explore). By contrast, the babies born to mothers with a normal protein diet benefitted from the enriched living conditions. Diamond concluded that the protein-rich diet was vital to the growth of healthy nerve cells, ones which can respond positively to our living conditions. As far as the brain is concerned, there are several other important ingredients in a balanced diet, including the B vitamins, sources of choline (e.g. soya beans, egg yolks, and peanuts), and antioxidants (e.g. through vitamin C and vitamin E sources, such as blueberries and strawberries). Again, these different aspects of mental and physical functioning tend to interact, as in an exercise regime fostering healthy eating.

## *Novelty*

"There is reason to believe that learning ... pragmatic skills produces specific as well as general benefits."[4] For example, if older adults were required to learn useful life skills (e.g. digital photography) they may experience a significant increase in their working memories. A further benefit, in addition to learning a new skill, is that the adults also learn about learning itself. This means that they have a recipe for continuing to develop new skills in the future, thus continuing to keep their brains working effectively.

It has been estimated that over 5 million Americans now have Alzheimer's disease, a disease that is the seventh leading cause of death across all ages in the US, and the fifth most common cause of death in Americans aged 65 and older.[5] The existence of milder forms of the kinds of the problems that characterize Alzheimer's is thought to be much higher, including slight problems in thinking (such as difficulty recalling information, expressing ideas in language, and other mental activities that do not yet interfere with daily living). What can be done to delay or even reverse these cognitive declines? Latterly, psychologists and others have identified several ways of altering the older adult's lifestyle to minimize these problems. They include physical exercise (see below), mental stimulation, stress reduction, and life-skills training. One of the benefits of the digital age is that it can act as a stimulus for brain activity, and one study found that older adults who surfed the Internet increased their brain activity, particularly in those bits of the brain (the pre-frontal cortex) that are associated with problem solving and decision making, which are particularly valuable skills. One implication of this recent research relates to the learning of computer-based skills. That is, you may be retired and have absolutely no problems with your mental performance, but if you have not yet learnt how to do things like surf the Internet (and use emails to communicate with your friends and family), now may be a good time to acquire these skills (see the case study in Chapter 5). Another research finding is that older adults who are not part of what is called the "digital native group" (young people who grew up with computers) may need to press on with acquiring those skills, as many older adults are now doing, to protect themselves against declining brain power.[6] Not only has it been estimated that it takes older adults twice as long as younger adults to learn such new technologies, they also tend to make more errors when interacting with the devices, particularly ones that have small key pads or screens, such as smart phones. There may also be a growing attitudinal resistance to using new technologies, so again it is probably better to start sooner rather than later.

Of course, this new learning will build on prior learning and there is reason to believe that the years of education and mental development that one has acquired will affect the ability to benefit from new experiences and to minimize the risk of these mental problems or of Alzheimer's disease itself. There is reason to believe that the more complex and well-developed the brain, the better it is able to stave off problems. A related finding is that the more complex and novel the new technology the more likely it is to be of benefit to the brain. This can be thought to interact with prior learning, in that those with a modicum of technological sophistication are more likely to move on to the more complex and challenging areas. However, it is only right to acknowledge that research in the area of dementia generally has not yet reached the point at which we can say with confidence that these different activities have a clear-cut effect. Rather, they are probably best regarded as promising ways to play an active role, so that at least you can feel good about attempting to resist and decline.

## Challenging the Brain

You are on a long car journey and with surprise realize that you have been "miles away" for some time, driving along on "autopilot." Or when you play your sport you occasionally enter another, magical world, a space where everything seems effortless and joyful. It can take a while to get back to normality. These are everyday examples of what our brains can do when properly channeled into the "zone" or similar "altered states of consciousness." We will all have had this kind of experience at some time or another, though you may well not have attempted to reach that state deliberately. Only a few rather specialized human beings will consciously get "into the zone," such as artists, top athletes, and those who practice meditation (especially "dynamic meditation" – i.e. meditation on the move), Yoga, or similar "self-control" methods (e.g. Buddhist monks). What exactly is this zone, and how can we get into it?

Studies of the zone (the "zone of optimal functioning") can be found in sport psychology, where quotes from famous athletes recount how they achieved their finest moments while occupying a cocoon-like level of absorption in their game, a deeper kind of concentration. Here are the main features of the zone state, starting with concentration (to which we will return):

- Appropriate concentration, often referred to in sport as having the "right focus."
- Being in the right state of arousal, energized but relaxed, often called "intensity."
- Feeling confident about one's ability, so that self-doubt is not a distracting issue.
- In control of one's action, without feeling that one has to force anything (the "8 out of 10" rule: even when you want maximum power, proceed with only 80 percent effort).
- A positive preoccupation with what is happening, and everything that surrounds it (e.g. reframing adverse events so as to channel them into one's own improved performance: "there was bound to be a setback – stay focused").
- Determination and commitment (force the doubts away and point the mind back at the points above).

When in this zone state, we will also tend to have a number of physical feelings, such as feeling loose and relaxed, rather than tight and tense; we'll feel solid, balanced and strong, rather than shaky, unsteady, and weak. Our limbs will feel light and energetic, while our actions will appear effortless, fluid and smooth. By contrast, when we are in what sport psychologists call a "choking" state we will feel heavy, tired, self-conscious, and awkward. Accompanying these physical feelings are characteristic psychological ones. Whereas during a choking phase we may feel scared, panicked, rushed, confused, and overloaded, in the zone we will tend to feel powerful, calm, tranquil and eerily peaceful, with clear and readily-focused thoughts, often on a very simple aspect of effective performance (e.g. moving smoothly). As noted in this chapter's case study (below), such states can also occur doing mundane domestic tasks: "Life slows down and you have more time: instead of hurrying a job you do it properly and get more satisfaction out of it."

Unfortunately, this zone state is often a fleeting experience; in particular, it is a state that is extremely difficult to create voluntarily, particularly when we most need it (e.g. when "choking"). The best avenue that I know is called "the inner game."

## The "Inner Game"

Thankfully, there is at least one way to gain some influence over the zone, so that you stand a better chance of entering it when you wish to. This allows you to gain much greater enjoyment from your sport, and similarly from retirement and other parts of your life. Here's what the author, Tim Gallwey, says about the zone and the inner game:

> Concentration is the most important skill, both for outer and inner games. Nothing of excellence is achieved without it. It is the primary ingredient of the learning process and the foundation of all true enjoyment. Yet it is one of the least studied and understood of all our innate capabilities.[7]

Although concerned with sport, the inner game is a philosophy that extends to all manner of activities, especially ones that have relaxed concentration at their core. Surely one of the most common applications comes in terms of coping with daily stress, and there is an inner game book devoted to that (see Recommended Reading). For instance, what is the inner game of cutting the grass, driving into town, or doing the weekly shop? In *The Art of Travel* De Botton notes how travel heightens self-awareness, through showing us our own reflections in the things that we observe: "A momentous but until then overlooked fact was making its first appearance: that I had inadvertently brought myself with me to the island."[8] Travel can also help us to question what we know about a place, what we expect, or what we would like to know, prompting us on "the importance of having the right question to ask of the world."[9] This philosophy leads to the idea that, in contrast to the traditional gifts for those unfortunate enough to have stayed at home, we might better come back with a fresh perspective: "we might return from our journeys with a collection of small, unfeted but life-enhancing thoughts."[10] Through such a process, we might glimpse what life is all about, or sense the path to our own happiness: "If our lives are dominated by a search for happiness, then perhaps few activities reveal as much about the dynamics of this quest ... than our travels."[11] This might include unrealistic expectations (e.g. that being on vacation should make one feel happy), aspects of how we relate to others (we might be exceptionally self-centered on vacation), or significant disappointment when things refuse to go to plan (perhaps because we are rushing?). The real challenge is to learn from such experiences, aided by travelling, so that ultimately travel ceases to matter. De Botton quotes Pascal: "The sole cause of man's unhappiness is that he does not know how to stay quietly in his room."[12] This has been recycled in recent times into the saying that "the need for vacations is due to a lack of imagination." Room-travel is the best destination: profit from journeying the familiar routes, but with better concentration! To help you consider this interesting angle on life, Gallwey[13] helpfully breaks concentration down into phases:

- *Awareness-raising*: Gallwey has a series of ingenious exercises that he uses in sport to help the athlete become more aware of what helps to produce excellence, such as attention to the feelings in the key muscle groups during successful performance (kinesthetic awareness). For instance, my golf coach is encouraging me to notice how my weight transfers as I strike the ball, to attend to how my arms sweep around my neck and my right shoulder ends up pointing to the left-hand side. In other parts of life we might attend to the success of everyday movements (e.g. walking or dressing), trying to notice what is going on in our muscles (e.g. which ones are working hardest?).

- *Discrimination*: This involves deepening our grasp on the key aspects of the action, such as how those muscles feel when a performance is deemed to be especially good. Our state of mind should be curious, fascinated with details of things we thought we understood. The idea is one of enquiring into what is happening and being absorbed in that process of self-observation. For instance, can you begin to discriminate between the "better" movements, in terms of felt qualities like smoothness or continuity? This may involve a helpful image, encouraging ideas of effortlessness or smoothness.

- *Programming*: As your concentration improves, experiment with different ways of thinking, so as to identify an optimal approach. In sport a classic example is the "pre-shot routine," in which a golfer (for example) will prepare to hit the ball by going through a number of preliminary steps (e.g. identify a target; visualize how the ball will travel there; waggle; swing nice and easy). This is usually associated with positive self-talk, as in talking oneself through these steps. What makes sense in your experiment? What feels comfortable and promising?

- *Let it happen*: The final part of facilitating this kind of experiential learning is to encourage yourself to trust: to try and engage your autopilot and give it full authority to fly your performance plane. Your focus is not on critically evaluating how things are going, but rather on calmly watching how they are unfolding, with careful but unflustered observation, with amused curiosity.

## Exercise: Healthy Body, Healthy Mind

As those who take regular exercise will usually report enthusiastically, there are immediate and lasting benefits to keeping the body suitably active. If you do not already take regular exercise, and wish to so do, then the sensible precaution is to first check-in with your Doctor, ideally with some idea of the proposed exercise program and your personal goals.

What are those benefits? During exercise we can feel the joy of moving well (e.g. when performing techniques within a sport); the buzz of competition; the release of tension; the contrast with sitting at home (especially if in the fresh air, in beautiful surroundings); the fun of pitting one's wits against the task, the elements or environment (e.g. hill-walking); the satisfaction of learning new things; the exhilaration of performing an action successfully (especially if it results in a great result); not to mention social participation and the sense of belonging that can follow (most obviously in team activities, or when we operate in unison to music, such as a fitness class). Additionally, exercise usually results in relaxation and inner calm, heightened self-esteem (especially if we have been worrying about our physical wellbeing or doubting our competence); a sense of accomplishment; the satisfaction of staying in reasonable shape; mood enhancement (beating the blues); stress management; improved hardiness, Stoicism and resilience; and extra self-confidence. (See Figure 7.1)

If you think about something like a fitness class, exercise typically involves a sequence of suitably varied activities, which can be thought of as small, successive challenges, each with explicit goals (e.g. to perform a particular Pilates movement smoothly). With practice, a full hour of strenuous yet synchronized activity can be mastered, one that may have seemed impossible at first. In addition, by working under the direction of an instructor, we have a demonstration of what we are supposed to be doing (and showing us that it can be done: see Table 3.1) alongside a class of peers of varied ability imitating that movement. This means that there's usually someone

**Figure 7.1**   Gentle exercise brings several benefits such as raising your mood

else in the group with whom we can identify, and alongside whom we can measure our progress. This social dimension is important, making it more likely that we will persist, while giving a sense of being joined together in this effort, perhaps orchestrated by appropriate music, in a stimulating physical environment. We are also away from our usual stressors, representing a welcome haven. Under these circumstances, the effort achieved may well exceed what we could have managed on our own, teaching us about things like our untapped potential, tolerance of discomfort, and tenacity. As this hopefully illustrates, these elements of a fitness class can alter our perceptions of our physical ability (e.g. improving our strength and balance), develop our coping strategies (e.g. tackling specific physical problems), and provide social support (e.g. reality contact and a sense of belonging) in a way that can boost our self-confidence and leave us with the warm, satisfied glow of achievement.

Longer term, there is another significant benefit for your health: "If physical exercise were a drug it would be hitting the headlines."[14] This conclusion was based on a review of more than 60 studies of exercise and cancer, which suggested that exercise not only increases energy but also significantly helps the body to combat the disease (those who took at least 150 minutes of moderate exercise a week were 40 percent less likely to suffer a recurrence or to die from the disease).[15] Exercise has also been found to decrease the risk of cardiovascular disease, alongside all other causes of mortality (i.e. it prolongs life); it reduces physical frailty (by slowing the decline in bone density and muscle-mass); and it raises quality of life (e.g. by increasing independence and activity options).

When exercise is part of sport then its significance can be profound, as illustrated by this example from the rugby star Jonny Wilkinson's autobiography.[16] When he took a summer off from international rugby in 2002 he thought it would recharge his batteries. Instead, he found himself thinking about life without rugby, finding everything pointless. He came to realize that rugby represented a means to test and improve himself, without which his very identity was questioned. Such experiences will no doubt make some readers incredulous: after all, it's just a game. Although objectively true, such a perception badly underestimates the subjective meaning that exercise or sport can have for individuals. Sport, like life, is what one makes of it: "To see the world in a grain of sand, and to see heaven in a wild flower, hold infinity in the palm of your hands, and eternity in an hour."[17] Indeed, many in sport have viewed it as life in microcosm: for those who would see, it is a rich source of learning, whether about imagination or discipline; and it is a superb arena for personal development. As Tim Gallwey put it, "games are pretend realities ... in which you can experiment and take risks without great penalties for failure ... and an expression of skill for the sake of excellence. It can be art."[18] In short, all that life can throw at you, the stressors and the frustrations, the highs and the lows: they await you in sport, life's laboratory for athletic excellence: the interminable struggle to cope, to get to the point where you are accepted as a player; and perhaps most vital of all, a commitment to self-improvement within a harsh arena, full of aggression, game-playing, bad luck, and downright cheating. In the end it is not the improvement that makes sport so special, it is the process of improving. As one coach put it: "Big improvements require working and chipping away for years ... The process, not the end result, enriches life ... every day is another opportunity to chase ... dreams. I want them to come to the end of their days with smiles on their faces, knowing that they did all they could with what they had."[19]

At the time of writing, a neat illustration of some of the benefits of gentle exercise has been published.[20] It compares Yoga against routine medical care by a general practitioner (GP). Exercise treatments are now widely used, but typically they only have a small effect. It was thought that Yoga may work better, as it combines exercise with a mental focus, self-awareness, self-care, and relaxation. In particular, there is evidence that Yoga can be effective in treatment of lower back pain, but prior research has utilized small samples and a short-term follow-up period. In the study to be described, 313 adults with chronic or recurrent low back pain were allocated randomly to usual GP care (157) or Yoga (12 classes, over 3 months, delivered by 12 teachers). Both groups received a back pain education booklet and the study took place in 39 general practices in different regions of England, from Manchester to Cornwall. Participants were 18–65 years of age, and had visited their GP in the last18 months due to low back pain. About 5 percent of the participants were unemployed, but none were defined as retired, though some were not seeking employment. The average duration of back pain problems was in region of 10 years. Yoga took place at non-medical venues and consisted of an introduction to the basic elements of Yoga, adapted for back pain (e.g. "asana" and "pranyama"). This included relaxing, seated and supine poses, education on posture and up to 15 minutes of relaxation training. Classes lasted for 75 minutes, and took place 12 times (i.e. weekly). Class members were given a manual and a relaxation CD, covering guided relaxation, color meditation, breath awareness, and mental positivity. In addition to attending the classes, students were encouraged to do 30 minutes of Yoga daily, using the CD. By contrast, the "usual GP care" was not detailed; I assume it included reassurance, pain-killing medication, and practical advice. The authors concluded that Yoga yielded greater improvements in back function than routine GP care over the study's one-year period, and was also safe and cost-effective.

For those with a depressed quality of life, controlled research on mood disorders has suggested that exercise can be as effective as an antidepressant, with the additional bonus of lasting benefits if the exercise is maintained. A review of studies that evaluated the effects of exercise on mood led to suggestions that exercise should be incorporated within therapy for anxiety and depression.[21] There is a direct benefit in relation to anxiety, as the symptoms of exercise and anxiety can overlap (e.g. raised pulse, perspiration, dizziness). In this sense, exercise can afford a way of recognizing that such symptoms need not be signs of anything frightening (e.g. a heart attack, going mad), reducing over time the likelihood that anxiety sufferers will panic at these symptoms. In the case of depression, it appears that exercise mobilizes vital brain chemicals (e.g. serotonin), and may also help by improving sleep.

The quantity of exercise and quality of life are naturally linked, as illustrated by a study of jogging and cycling through middle age conducted in Toronto in 2011. The study suggested that this exercise could "stop the biological clock and delay aging by up to 12 years, whilst boosting energy levels, coordination, balance, and muscle power."[22] These benefits are especially relevant to those of us who are growing old, being the most sedentary segment of the population. In 2006,[23] a survey in England revealed that only 40 percent of men and 28 percent of women reached the recommended weekly physical activity target (i.e. at least 30 minutes of moderate to vigorous activity at least five times per week: vigorous to raise the pulse to 120 beats per minute) and this overall figure decreased with age. These figures dropped to 20 percent and 17 percent, respectively, between the ages of 65 and 74, yet older adults stand to benefit most from exercise! This is a striking paradox: despite the strong evidence for mental and physical benefits, relatively few people take exercise seriously (a recent survey in the US[24] indicated that 25 percent of the population took no proper exercise at all). Of those who mean well, the initial discomfort and low pay-off will typically destroy their New Year resolution. This reminds me of the cartoon showing a doctor and a retired patient. The doctor says: "What suits your busy schedule better, exercising for an hour a day, or being dead for 24 hours a day?"

More seriously, low motivation for exercise is a crucial challenge, so those starting out need to achieve success. It is therefore important to start out intelligently (e.g. a gentle program, aimed at immediate benefits, like heightened mood and reduced tension). The "big pay-off" opportunities are often the very ones that get skipped: when you have a headache take exercise, not aspirin, and so forth. Weight loss, lowered cholesterol levels, and similar benefits are only suitable as medium-term goals. Having some social commitment is a significant motive for many, as in joining a group that meets at a regular time and place, and committing to be there. A good example is "the University of the Third Age" (U3A), an international self-help organization for retired people, which puts on regular walks (as well as many other stimulating activities, within "learning cooperatives" where members take turns to teach and to learn).

Another important recent finding is that all exercise can be beneficial, not just those big efforts in the gym. A study conducted at University College London indicated that even light, occasional exercise carries benefits. For example, just 20 minutes of weekly walking, housework, or gardening was shown to raise mood.[25] However, the opposite also applies, in that people may trade-off high and low exercise periods, getting no net benefit. One study randomly allocated 464 overweight women who did not exercise to either a personal trainer to follow an exercise plan or a control condition (i.e. stay inactive). Both groups were to stick to their usual diet. By the end of the trial the researchers found very little difference in weight, as those who exercised felt tired and so did less for the rest of day (e.g. taking the lift, rather than walking).[26]

In a second related study, over 400,000 men and women from Taiwan were followed over an eight-year period.[27] Based on the intensity and duration of their weekly physical activity programs, they were classified as inactive (i.e. less than 1 hour of exercise per week), low (90 minutes of exercise a week or 15 minutes a day), medium (e.g. brisk walking), high (e.g. jogging), or very high activity (e.g. vigorous running). Of the 20,000 plus older adult participants (60 years or older), 43 percent fell into the inactive category. The researchers found that, compared with those in the inactive group, those in the low activity group had a 14 percent reduced risk of premature death (from any cause) and 3 years more life expectancy. Every additional 15 minutes of daily exercise beyond the minimum figure of 15 minutes a day reduced mortality by 4 percent. This effect is huge: equivalent in scale to a nation stopping smoking (e.g. one in nine deaths prevented). These benefits applied to all age groups and both sexes, as well as to those with cardiovascular disease. One reason this study is significant is because the usual standard of 30 minutes a day, 5 days a week is hard to achieve for many (a third of the American adult population meet this standard, but less than 20 percent in East Asian countries like China do so). A "minimum dose" of 15 minutes of moderate intensity daily exercise is more achievable and still carries significant health benefits. What's more, once people start exercising, they tend to exercise more, notice a decrease their weight, and identify other benefits, leading to a virtuous cycle.

There are other physical motives for exercising. According to Marian Diamond,[28] there is growing evidence that the absence of exercise presents the individual with a number of health risks (e.g. diabetes and heart problems). As far as the brain is concerned, one of exercise's key functions is to ensure a good supply of oxygen to the brain. As we age, our blood vessels become less efficient and so it becomes keenly important to ensure that a sufficient supply of oxygen gets through the brain and feeds all of the vital areas. An example of research on the relationship between exercise and the older brain was conducted by some Canadian researchers in 2010.[29] They recruited 67 older adults (men and women, average age of 68 years) and assigned them to an experimental group or a control group. Those in the experimental group engaged in a 3-month fitness training program. Both groups were made up of people with good health status. In the exercise group, there were three one-hour long training sessions each week, involving stretching, fast walking, and aerobic dancing. There were adequate warm-up and cool-down periods, and a progressive increment in the exercise duration and energy expenditure. In time, participants were able to exercise vigorously for 40 minutes per session. Not only did the participants in the experimental, aerobic training group improve their cardiorespiratory capacity significantly, they also showed improvements in brain functioning. The latter was assessed using a reaction time assessment, something that assesses how long it takes an individual to press a button in relation to different stimuli presented on a screen. The speed and accuracy of responding were calculated, alongside errors. In addition to a 25 percent improvement in physical fitness in the 3-month period, the participants in the experimental group also showed the expected improvements in their reaction time performances, indicating an association between physical fitness and better brain performance. In particular, this reaction time task required controlled and quite subtle cognitive processing, including the skill of preparing to make a response (which requires an ability to assess the likelihood that a particular stimulus will appear on the screen). There were also indications of better concentration, and these effects were most marked for those who began the program with the lowest levels of fitness. The authors concluded that fitness work may afford a protective buffer against age-related brain decline. Evidence from brain scanning studies suggest that this boost to the brain is probably due to improved cardiovascular functioning, that is, the improved fitness reaches key brain regions associated with our ability to concentrate and consider how to make quick responses to situations. Other research indicates that exercise protects brain cells from death, improves the concentration of nutrients in the brain (e.g. oxygen and glucose), as well as the expanding and contracting movement of the brain's blood vessels, which benefits its cells.[30] For such reasons, "exercise appears to reduce the risk of dementia by 32 percent, provided it takes place three or more times a week, lasts at least 20 minutes, is vigorous, causing breathlessness and sweating."[31] It also improves mental performance generally (but especially coordination and planning), sometimes by large amounts, but it appears that such mental benefits require at least 30 minutes of strenuous activity, somewhere between three to five times a week.

The importance of a healthy lifestyle was emphasized in one of the most comprehensive studies on the causes of cancer, conducted in 2011 by Professor Parkin at London University.[32] He analyzed data on cancer cases occurring in the UK, concluding that nearly half could have been prevented by a healthier lifestyle (40 percent of cancer cases in women; 45 percent in men). The leading cause was smoking, which accounted for 23 percent of cancers in men, 16 percent in women: these were mostly lung cancers (86 percent of instances), but also included cancers of the stomach, liver, and pancreas (22 percent of Britons smoke). The next most risky aspect of how we live was obesity (6 percent of cancers), followed by not eating enough fruit and vegetables (5 percent). Eating too much red meat, salt, or insufficient fiber was also important in 5 percent of cancers, with alcohol implicated in 4 percent. Other causes included sunlight (4 percent), infections (3 percent), lack of exercise (2 percent), exposure to radiation (2 percent), or harmful chemicals at work, though these causes varied in their impact depending on the type of cancer (e.g. lack of exercise accounted for 3.4 percent of breast cancers). However, prostate cancer, which is the most common cancer among men in the UK, was not thought to be influenced by these factors and so was not thought to be preventable. It was concluded that "leading a healthy life does not guarantee that a person will not get cancer, but this study shows that healthy habits can significantly stack the odds in our favour."[33] This is a conclusion reached by researchers throughout the world, indicating the importance of healthy living habits.

After a tricky beginning, the case study that follows illustrates a balanced approach to retirement, including attention to diet and exercise.

## Case Study: Brian, being Exercised by Retirement

Brian had been the workshop superintendant for the county's ambulance service, responsible for the servicing of over 100 ambulances. Previously, Brian had completed his national service in the Army, including a period during 1953–4 serving in the "Communist War" in Malaya (part of the Cold War, in what is now called Malaysia; Malaya was a British Colony until 1957). This included playing the role of observer in spotter planes, trying to find Communist camps in the vast forests of Malaya. He would also throw out leaflets, designed to persuade the locals to change their ways. This work was at times risky and he was shot at, on one occasion returning with bullet holes in the wings of the plane. Although there must have been many frightening times, the army was actually a positive experience for Brian, who "became more confident." Although he had not wanted to join the army, "it was a period of my life that I would not have missed," because of the comradeship and travelling. He recalled being in tears when the time came to say farewell to his friends at the railway station. This army experience seemed to help him when started work in the ambulance garage as he did well there, soon coming off the floor to become the superintendent, with his "three pips."

## Retirement

At the age of 58, Brian retired from this management role. This was 22 years ago, and followed 30 years of service. It was "like a load lifted off my shoulders," as Brian had perceived the responsibility as a heavy burden, one that caused him to worry a lot: even at home over a weekend he "couldn't stop thinking" about his job and the problems of the moment.

Instead of treating this blessed relief from his burden as the end of his working life, Brian started to work in an unpaid capacity, in order to support his son's small business. He would go in to help most days of the week, until deciding that "enough was enough" some 7 years ago, at the age of 73. Brian had not been paid for this effort, as he wanted to help his son out. But it was "not what I wanted to do ... there were a hell of a lot of things that I wanted to do, especially travelling ... would like to have gone on a world tour ... still thinking I will do, but regretting jumping around like an idiot." So it was his conscience that had pricked him into this extended working life. On reflection, Brian also thought that he had committed so much of his time to this business "as a way of coping with the loss (of his wife): filling the time in," as a welcome distraction from mourning. Indeed, he would stay at work as late as possible, only leaving when the last person was ready to finish for the day. There was also a financial motive, in that he and his wife had helped to fund the purchase of their son's business by taking out a second mortgage.

*Life Events*

Now 80 years old, Brian's main concern is the feeling that his memory is beginning to fail him. This is the "foremost thing ... trying to remember." For example, he will ask himself "what the hell have I come in here for?," and to answer his own question he will often re-trace his steps through his house, only then remembering his mission. Another coping strategy used by Brian is to "go through the alphabet: usually works, if I've got the time." This is particularly bothersome to Brian as a "good memory plus the gift of the gab represents the best gift you can have." He notes in exasperation that he once knew the names of all 70 drivers who came to his workshop. Now he is perplexed at how, despite 30 years of knowing them, he can "stand there, seeing them in the street, thinking – what's their name?," and then end up "feeling a fool." Other examples are seeing somebody on television that he knows, and struggling far more than previously to recall their name. Another mental change that Brian is aware of is how time appears to "get quicker all the time," as in thinking that something that was actually several years ago had surely only occurred a few months ago.

However, his general physical health is currently good, having gone through a few operations and various other medical procedures (e.g. to tackle an enlarged prostate gland). He has made a strong recovery, and "on a good day" will regularly walk for over 2 miles along the sea front. This maintains his custom of regular and vigorous walks in the country, which peaked at 5-mile walks over rolling countryside. Brian also takes care over his diet: "Keep an eye on it ... vegetables and fruit ... fat taken off meat ... like a piece of cod."

*Coping*

In this last 7 years when he has been truly retired, Brian has coped by re-maining active: "always busy, pottering and mending things, or walking." He has two children and three grandchildren, two of whom he sees on a weekly or fortnightly basis. They are a comfort to him: "I like to see them ... they are affectionate." I asked Brian whether he reminisced with his own children and he replied that this was a definite feature with his daughter, who would often talk emotionally about her positive bond with her grandfather (who used to take her out every Saturday to her beloved horse riding). Not surprisingly, she was his favorite grandchild. He likes to hear from his daughter who will mostly phone (visiting them is partly a problem due to the 100 miles or so that separates them, but mainly because she has dogs which are a problem, as Brian doesn't like them jumping up on him or growling at him). As for his son, Brian keeps in regular touch, when he brings his daughters to see Brian: "nice to hear what he's doing ... usually about work." He noted that his children are "chalk and cheese" in that his son will listen, whereas his daughter "never comes up for breath."

I probed at Brian's fascination with travelling and it appeared to boil down to focusing on some long-standing ambitions, such as travelling down the Suez Canal, or visiting Australia. For Brian, the purpose behind the travelling seemed to be an interest or curiosity in these far-flung places, often arising from some kind of historical link to his own life, such as important news stories from the past.

### Positive Adjustment

Brian now feels "more content" with his life, having stopped worrying about work and done his bit for his children. He also enjoys a close relationship with his new partner, who has been a great help to him: "Oh yes, especially when I moved and had my operations ... if it hadn't been for her, I would have been in a state, housework, meals, she's been fantastic." His partner is also more outgoing than he is, helpfully encouraging him to participate in daily activities of some kind (e.g. visiting shopping or gardening centers). I asked Brian whether he felt that his growing maturity had brought wisdom or contentment? He said that "Life slows down and you have more time: instead of hurrying a job you do it properly and get more satisfaction out of it." By comparison, in the past he would have thought that a job could be finished once it was "near enough" fixed. He generally gets "some satisfaction from doing things well" and smiled at the example of "beating manufacturers by repairing things that couldn't be fixed" (in the manufacturer's opinion). He also readily noted frustrations, such as "getting irritated with people," like other drivers ("Why the hell didn't he indicate?", "Look at that fool, overtaking on that bend"). This is an aspect of himself that he feels has become worse over the years: "hate self for it." He also regrets going into his post-retirement "job" of helping out his son with his new business. Although he feels good about the gesture that he made, he also regrets not having commenced his travelling plans at that stage, when he was in a better physical shape and so could have enjoyed the experience more. Taken together with a strong sense that his peers are steadily passing away, he can sometimes feel quite gloomy: "all doom and gloom ... for example, 70 drivers and they're starting to thin out."

## Conclusions

Although tradition dictates a rather damning view of retirement (all decline and despair), in this chapter I have highlighted several clear examples of continuing development and a meaningful progression during our third age. There are many potential activities that spur this development, but I focused on "E" for exercise because of its clear illustration of these core principles: "use it or lose it" (i.e. the brain's need of novelty and challenge); "healthy body, healthy mind" (e.g. the role of diet; the ways our body and mind interact, illustrated by Yoga); and "healthy mind, healthy body" (how concentration enhances our functioning, especially the fascinating business of the "zone," accessed through the "inner game"). If anything, it appears that we have traditionally underestimated the importance of lifestyle for wellbeing, not just in what we would nowadays regard as the "obvious" links between exercise and physical health, but also the value to our mental health of a lifestyle that incorporates recreation, relaxation, time in Nature (getting out into the hills and the woods, for peace perspective, and wisdom), religious or spiritual involvement, and service to others. Many of these are free, readily available, have no side-effects, yet can seemingly match modern medical treatments. It seems obvious that we should give them greater attention.

The case study of Brian illustrates someone doing just that as his years went by, as well as touching on several chapter themes (such as aiming for excellence), nicely capturing the "purpose" aspect of the RECIPE for thriving in retirement. Brian's life's purpose centered on family life and later on his son's business, but in a belated retirement Brian has clearly developed his own interests, including travel, staying active, and having valued relationships (e.g. his partner and grandchildren). Through all of this experience the bright beam of coping shines, that is, it is through our adaptive efforts that we develop. Although this chapter focused on E for exercise it also covered other aspects of the RECIPE.

# 8

# Conclusions

*Happiness is not the absence of problems, but the ability to deal with them.*[1]

In this final chapter I want to conclude my account of retirement by discussing what many would regard as its goal: happiness. When Britain's Prime Minister, David Cameron, launched his "happiness index" in November 2010, he announced that his government would henceforth measure quality of life alongside the traditional indicators, such as economic growth. Happiness is to be assessed in terms of people's health, education, and environment, to offer a more comprehensive assessment "of measuring a country's progress."[2] I rejoice at the Prime Minister's wisdom. Like sleep, happiness has an elusive quality when we try to control it, yet it is something for which we yearn, so how can we best foster it? I will look at the traditional answer, wealth, consider several other factors, but dwell on wisdom as a more achievable goal. After presenting the case study of Dominic, who found his happiness in racing cars, I will summarize the essence of my RECIPE for successful retirement, drawing on the material within the whole book.

To set the scene, recall that the traditional view of ageing is fairly pessimistic. Thankfully, public perceptions of the older adult have become more positive in recent times, but there are undoubtedly some major obstacles to happiness during retirement. While life expectancy has risen dramatically over the last few centuries (with the anticipation that this trend will continue over the next few decades), the quality of life in retirement has not kept pace. Chronic medical conditions, financial concerns, or excessively

*The Psychology of Retirement: Coping with the Transition from Work*, First Edition. By D. Milne.
© 2013 D. Milne. Published 2013 by John Wiley & Sons, Ltd.

high expectations may all play a part in what for many turns into a struggle. What can be done to promote a happier, more successful retirement?

## Happiness

Happiness is usually defined as a personal sense of general wellbeing, characterized by positive feelings from doing the right things (ethical action) or from wanting for nothing else (completeness). The definition pivots on how we feel, ranging from the absence of pain or suffering to enjoying good health and a sense of wellbeing. Although much sought after (for some it signifies the worth of a life), it is an elusive state that appears rarely and when we least expect it. If it occurs at all, we might glimpse it in momentary episodes of inner calm, amusement, understanding, or compassion. If fortunate, we may even go further up this happiness spectrum, to slightly more enduring if even more elusive states, like joy, rapture, or euphoria ("jumping for joy," a "light heart," "pure bliss"). The intensity of any feeling of happiness can be thought of in different forms. For example, in his book, *The Examined Life,*[3] the American philosopher Robert Nozick thought there was what I will term "circumstantial happiness" (i.e. arising simply because of circumstances, such as being newly-wed or inheriting money), "process happiness" (i.e. arising from being pleasurably involved in relating to people, places or things) and "life satisfaction" (i.e. feeling pleased with the way life has turned out overall). He thought that each state was associated with different intensities of happiness, and it is also clear that there are differing durations.

There is also a complex thinking dimension to happiness, including having benchmarks or expectations (to allow us to evaluate) and making meaning about our lives, often through viewing our lives as part of something bigger, as in raising a family or the Christian's life purpose of "glorifying God." Other aspects of such thinking are being the best that we can be (e.g. through concentrating so intensely that we become absorbed and "at one" with our focus), and generally by living "the good life," as in seeking sound reasoning and a clear understanding (e.g. to limit fear and foolishness and to develop wisdom).

In addition to how we feel and think, happiness depends on our taking the "right" action. In particular, the collective wisdom on acting well concentrates on doing good, in terms of acting ethically (i.e. in being fair or just). While this might underpin our happiness, there is reason to view actions on a scale, from engaging in simple pleasures through to accomplishments and personal excellence that bring recognition or private joy. Perhaps one of the main reasons for the popularity of religion is that it systematically unites these subtle thoughts, feelings, and behaviors, fostering a sense of belonging and happiness.

As "happiness" is a particularly vague and subjective feeling, many prefer other terms: "general life satisfaction," "wellbeing," or "quality of life." These are more firmly based on what is important to us all, such as work, health, and relationships. This is often related to our material status (e.g. wealth, property), but it also depends crucially on how well off we think we are, relatively speaking. If we combine these qualities, happiness is:

- Finding meaning in your life (e.g. through projects, spirituality, religion, or voluntary work).
- Being pleasurably involved in relating to people, places, or things (i.e. absorbed concentration).
- Experiencing positive attitudes and emotions (e.g. gaining satisfaction through achievement in a career or from raising a family).
- Enjoying good social relationships (especially through intimate ones, but also through social support).
- Having physical and mental health (enough to engage in the above; free from pain or suffering).
- Enjoying material sufficiency (enough finances and other resources to meet your needs).

One of the surprising things about happiness is how fleeting and elusive it is, in the sense that you could be engaged in several of the things listed above, but go for months without a distinct moment when you felt truly happy. Taking into account circumstances and our general mood or personality (in the sense that we may have a happy or depressed disposition), this alerts us to a crucial idea: that happiness is not something that can be arranged or controlled, like reaching a destination at a particular time. Nor do we necessarily achieve happiness once we retire, any more than we do when we marry, start a new job, or become a lottery winner. These are simply transitions that may promote happiness, but which will soon evaporate if we do not manage the situation well. Specifically, happiness appears to emerge from how we live our lives; as Robert Nozick put it, happiness "rides piggyback on other things that are positively evaluated."[4] It depends on a process, one that requires a certain way of experiencing life via positive attitudes, a sense of purpose and social involvement. In this sense, happiness is as much about our attitudes to living as it is to our circumstances or health. Judging from the first National Wellbeing Survey of 80,000 adults in the UK (reported in 2012), these things may interact.[5] The survey indicated that those aged 65 and over were the happiest, especially men. Other circumstances that were positively associated with happiness were being recently married (or recently joined in a civil partnership, both of which scored 7.7 out of a possible 10), having children, and working part-time. Geographic differences were also apparent, suggesting cultural or environmental influences: those living in Scotland and Northern Ireland registered the highest happiness scores. Least happy were divorced males aged 45–50 living in London. Similar findings emerged from a survey of nearly 350,000 Americans. In this study, enjoyment of life began to increase at 40, continuing until it peaked at 85. This positive association between age and happiness was thought to be due to an attitude of acceptance, one of being increasingly satisfied with what we have.[6]

This attitude of acceptance has also been identified in research on brain injuries. It has suggested that the more serious the injury, the higher the life satisfaction, a surprising finding and one that supports the idea that an attitude of acceptance may be important. One study tried to understand how this can occur.[7] Over 600 people who had had moderate-to-severe accidents that caused a brain injury completed a form. The results indicated that having a strong sense of identity, seeing oneself as a survivor, having adequate social support and improved relationships following the accident all played a part in increasing life satisfaction. A curious finding was that those who had experienced the worst injuries tended to report the greatest satisfaction, which the researchers attributed to these brain-injured people having a greater appreciation of surviving and developing a stronger sense of their identity (e.g. as a "survivor"), a positive sense of themselves which assisted their relationships.

Happiness also emerges from the way we approach life. This is illustrated by the realization that even basic, everyday work tasks can become a source of happiness. According to the account in Alain De Botton's book, *The Pleasures and Sorrows of Work* "the Protestant worldview, as it developed over the sixteenth century, attempted to redeem the value of everyday tasks, proposing that many apparently unimportant activities could in fact enable those who undertook them to convey the qualities of their souls. In this schema, humility, wisdom, respect and kindness could be practiced in a shop no less sincerely than in a monastery."[8] This "happiness attitude" fundamentally continues a lifelong commitment to growth and development, to making the most of our situation, but also of doing our best for others. This social dimension is captured in the concept of "flourishing," which places our personal happiness in a social context. It can be measured with questionnaires, such as the "Psychological Flourishing Scale,"[9] which includes the following statements:

I lead a purposeful and meaningful life.
I am engaged and interested in my daily activities.
I actively contribute to the happiness and wellbeing of others.
I generally trust others and feel part of my community.
People respect me.

As these statements indicate, happiness seems to arise from meaningful engagement in life, from a firm material foundation, embedded in a supportive social network. Reflecting this perspective, great therapists have offered opinions like: "Pursuing happiness as an end in itself is doomed to failure ... it is only achieved incidentally, as a by-product of seeking meaning" (e.g. through compassionate acts or concern for the wellbeing of others).[10] Therefore, happiness seems to happen when we forget about ourselves and about trying to be happy, occurring especially when we are acting ethically, wisely and with compassion. At such times we may feel a rather special mental peace, a calm detachment from self-centered needs and desires. This view is supported by the findings from The Longevity Project, which has followed the lives of 1,500 people since 1921:

> The people who lived the longest generally were those who had the most interesting and productive lives. They were satisfied with what they had achieved. True joy generally came from maturity, not from spur of the moment indulgences ... the pursuit of happiness is best thought of as the pursuit of accomplishment; not money, but the pursuit of deep involvement with others and of meaningful achievement.[11]

There appears to be a further contributor to happiness, illustrated by research reported in the popular press at the time of writing.[12] If we consider these general statements to how we live minute-by-minute, we can begin to glimpse how happiness is constructed. By nature, the human mind is a wandering mind, a mind which naturally flits from one thing to another, so we rarely absorb ourselves fully in the present. While this has many significant advantages (such as the ability to reason), it seems that we are happiest when the mind is focused on what we are doing, moment-by-moment. This view is reflected in many of the great philosophical ideas and religious traditions, which suggest that happiness is found in the "here and now," by living intensely in the moment, so that our current experience is deepened and enriched. An example is meditation, but there are other examples of mental absorption such as focusing on a hobby, task, or skill. Such moments can bring a special kind of feeling, a contentedness, a happy episode in our experience of life. Two psychologists at Harvard University studied happiness by contacting over 2,000 adults on their iPhones at random times, asking them to respond by saying what they were doing at that particular moment. They then rated their happiness on a scale, ranging from 0 (unhappy) to 100 (very happy). Finally, they were asked whether they were thinking about something other than what they were currently doing. The study confirmed three outcomes: their minds wandered half of the time; they were less happy during these unfocused times (regardless of what they were doing); and that, if they were focused on what they were doing, they consistently recorded high scores and were at their happiest. Concentrating was twice as important in causing them to feel happy, irrespective of how much they favored what they were doing. The psychologists concluded that: "a human mind is a wandering mind, and a wandering mind is an unhappy mind."[13]

We should also consider a popular source of happiness: money. Although not significant within the Longevity Project, does wealth not bring automatic happiness?

## Wealth and Happiness

Contrary to popular belief, money can help to buy happiness. The research evidence to support this comes from the strong correlation between life satisfaction and income. To illustrate, in one study, those with an income of less than US$10,000 rated their life satisfaction at about 6.5 on a 10-point scale.[14] By contrast, those who earned above US$200,000 had a satisfaction score that averaged above 7.5. It seems that this correlation is also a national phenomenon. A Gallup world survey conducted in 2006 used a scale of happiness called the "ladder of life." This survey asked people to rate where they were positioned, on the steps of an imaginary ladder that started with the worst life one can imagine for oneself (score 0) to the best life one can imagine (score 10). All of the poorer nations were relatively low on the ladder (scoring only 4 or 5 on the scale), whereas most of the wealthy nations were high on the scale, Nations with an average income of less than US$2,000 per year did not match any nation with an annual income of more than US$20,000 on the happiness scale: the lower the income, the poorer the happiness of the participants. Overall, the correlation between income and happiness turned out to be .82, a very high association. In summary, it is perhaps not surprising to note that those who live in rich nations are typically satisfied, whereas those in poorer nations tend not to be. There may be many reasons for this, but wealth would seem to be an important factor.

Even though there is this strong positive relationship between wealth and happiness, there are some notable exceptions. How might these be understood? Money is usually the result of our efforts, and we know that personal effectiveness (and the resulting sense of achievement) is an important ingredient in wellbeing, regardless of wealth. But there is also reason to believe in the "happy disposition," a feature of some personalities which appears to be in part genetic. A further reason for money being associated with happiness is through the social status that it tends to bring, perhaps by being linked to socially-valued activities such as developing a successful business or studying in order to build a profitable career. Similarly, good social standing can help us to feel good about ourselves and in turn influence the way that others relate to us (e.g. treated favorably, respected, and liked). Furthermore, the relationship between wealth and happiness can be due to the sense of personal control that money can give us, enabling us to be self-reliant and able to make decisions that favorably influence our lives: we can pay off debts and deal with negative concerns (like problems with our home or car), and we can be flexible about the things we most desire. To illustrate, researchers in New Zealand summarized over 600 studies that had been published on health, wealth and happiness, covering nearly half a million people from over 60 countries.[15] They concluded that the greatest source of happiness was feeling free to do as one pleased (see Figure 8.1), free to express oneself (provided that it did not go too far and alienate family and friends). At a more basic level, having money provides a secure feeling, a sense that we will be able to deal with a crisis should one arise (a "survival" need). Another reason is the simple pleasure that we can get from using money to buy goods or services ("retail therapy"). In conclusion, to quote Diener and Biswas-Diener, "Whether you have everything you ever wanted or live a simple life, you can be happy or unhappy, because process

**Figure 8.1**    Happiness can come from feeling free to do as you please

is the key."[16] One of their suggestions towards encouraging this process was "making wise choices." How might wisdom contribute to happiness?

## Wisdom

One of the qualities attributed to older people is wisdom, because their many life experiences have required reflection and promoted the development of understanding and insight. Sometimes wisdom is thought of purely in intellectual ways, such as a superior level of knowledge, observation, judgment, or advice ("philosophy" means the love of wisdom); while others suggest that wisdom entails a deeper and uncommon understanding of events, such as seeing through illusions to the truth, based on recognizing and accepting our human limitations (e.g. the constraints that aging can place on our physical functioning). Wisdom can also include values that are aimed at achieving a common good, by balancing competing pressures or viewpoints in order to determine the best course of action. There is also thought to be an emotional or affective dimension, including the ability to understand, empathize, and to be peaceful or gentle. Taken together, we can define wisdom as necessary in order to flourish. In keeping with the popular belief that older people are wiser, researchers in Michigan found that social reasoning improved with age.[17] They asked young, middle-aged, and older people from the local community to read stories about conflict (between people and groups) and predict how the conflicts would resolve. The older people showed a better understanding of the need to adopt several perspectives, to allow for compromise and to acknowledge the limits of our knowledge. These qualities neatly define "wisdom." The researchers concluded that older people should be assigned to key social roles involving intergroup negotiations.

Many studies have found a positive relationship between wisdom and life satisfaction, a sense of purpose and mastery, positive family relations, general adjustment to aging, an orientation towards personal growth, and positive social relations. Conversely, wisdom is minimally associated with depression and with avoiding thoughts about death or being frightened of death. Taken together, these findings suggest that wisdom promotes successful retirement, and has particular merit when situations are difficult and times are trying. Wisdom operates as a kind of coping resource, helping us to be more resilient and effective in applying what we have learnt to new crises. Part of that wisdom is seeing that life's trials and tribulations are necessary for us to appreciate the good times, and to foster happiness. Another is that there is value in modest living, simple pleasures, and limiting our desires. As the ancient Chinese sage Lao Tsu (translates as "old master") wrote in the sixth century, in *Tao Te Ching* (The Way):

> Retire when the work is done.
> This is the way of heaven.[18]

The case study of Dominic illustrates some of these points by demonstrating a wise decision about retirement.

# Case Study: Dominic, the Long-Suffering Motor Engineer

As a boy, Dominic's world was dominated by cars. Following in the footsteps of his father, a keen amateur engineer, he would tinker with old vehicles, gradually gaining competence in restoring them to full working order. From an early age he befriended the mechanic at the local garage. By the age of 14 he had enough competence to restore an old rusted wreck to full operation and near-original appearance, and when driving it proudly up and down on private roads, would have a beam of achievement on his face. This fascination led naturally to studying mechanical engineering at university, but this only lasted a year, as he realized it had been "the wrong choice . . . all maths and physics" moving him away from his beloved hands-on work with cars. He left academia and was apprenticed as a motor engineer for three years in a large, city-centre garage, followed by a period of employment as a mechanic before becoming self-employed at the age of 30. He remained self-employed as a mechanic for a further 32 years, gradually improving his premises from a railway archway to his own detached garage in the leafy suburbs. At the same time he also pursued a successful hobby as a racing car driver, becoming the national hill climb champion at the age of 29. On retiring as a mechanic aged 62, he decided that his present to himself should be a nice new fast car! This was the beginning of a successful retirement, something not to be taken for granted. We should therefore ask: what were the circumstances that allowed Dominic to make this successful transition, to be driving but not driven?

## Physical Wellbeing

Although in some respects his garage represented a comfortable workplace, there were some significant disadvantages. One critical factor was the lack of suitable facilities, particularly the absence of a ramp "to lift the car up in the air to a nice working height, which would have made many jobs much easier." This meant that, during the final 3 years, Dominic ended most days feeling "extremely sore," to the point that he could hardly walk. Each working day he was "almost crippled." Another factor was that he did the hard physical work without proper heating, partly as Dominic liked to keep his garage doors open. So he continued to work year in year out in a northerly region of the UK at what was the ambient air temperature. Some days "the spanners were so cold I could hardly hold them."

Adding to the physical ordeal, there was a strong sense of tiredness, such that, by the end of the working week, Dominic would be feeling "completely jiggered." One result of this was that half his weekend was lost to physical recovery. This became increasingly unbearable, resulting in a hernia at the age of 61, due to lifting while working on a car. This was in addition to a chronically sore back and sore knees. Things reached a point where he doubted his ability to continue. He recalled his alarm when his mother mentioned that he had several more years of work to do yet. His reaction was: "don't know if I can go on doing this." It became the case that every new job that came in represented bad news ("Oh God, not another one of those ... 3 days of agony"), while the thought of the next winter was getting him down. These negative thoughts were captured in a nightmare: "a long line of cars heading my way – would it be possible for me to do them all?"

Compounding the physical distress was Dominic's conscientiousness, a personality characteristic that meant that he found it difficult to disappoint his many regular customers ("can't let them down ... just have to do it"). He did, however, develop one helpful coping strategy, which was to sub-contract some of the work.

Then it happened that one day he was faced with fitting a new water pump to a Peugeot and he froze: "couldn't do it ... a sudden mental block ... don't know if I can do this," even though this was a job he'd done many times before. Somehow he continued to work, though he felt in a daze: "going through the motions while enduring a horrible feeling ... didn't want to be there, but couldn't understand what was happening." As far as Dominic was concerned, this was "the day I stopped." He started to tell everyone that he was winding down the business. Although in some ways this sounds like a panic attack, careful questioning suggested that it was more a case of reaching a significant realization, a psychological epiphany based on an increasingly unacceptable and aversive job. Completing his commitments was like scaling a "wall of loathing": he did complete all commitments but knew in his heart that this was the final lap.

### Critical Incident

Why was it only at this point, after years of physical suffering, that Dominic decided to quit? Only a couple of years earlier his brother, who was two-and-a-half years younger, had been pressured to retire and had accepted a redundancy package. Dominic had continued "working away," thinking that there was no such escape for him. Then one day his personal finance advisor asked him whether he had ever thought of retiring. As this advisor went through some of the options, the possibility became appealing to Dominic: he could sell his business, invest in an appropriate pension product, and retire now! "Eureka – could afford to quit ... just when everything was falling apart." Dominic decided to take one month off to sort out his business affairs and then fulfilled his existing obligations to customers, letting others know that he would be ceasing business on a specific date. With unusual assertiveness he told everyone that he was no longer able to do their car work and recommended another garage. With considerable relief, he then put a message on his answer-phone, saying "no longer in business." This represented a "big relief ... didn't have to work." For a while after retiring he just felt exhausted, "lazing around the house watching TV and doing very little all winter." Unlike some, Dominic reported feeling completely "chilled" about his new status, having no sense of let-down or discomfort about this unprecedented break.

## Social Support

He felt he had "suffered too much in silence ... no one to moan to ... might have helped" (Dominic had been married for nine years, but was single for most of his career). To illustrate, his mother was baffled by his dramatic decision to quit: she felt his garage provided "nice conditions." It is also perhaps significant that he worked alone. The importance of social support is underlined by the contrast he experienced when he got away from his solitary workplace to get vehicles an MOT certificate (i.e. road-worthiness). To take a car away from his own garage to someone else's place and to "have a blether [chat]" was an enjoyable break from the "lonely" garage, with only disc-jockeys Jimmy Young and Terry Wogan for company on the radio.

## Overview

Dominic's tale illustrates how employment is not necessarily something we need miss, especially if it has become an endurance test. It is striking how something as engrossing as his beloved motor car became aversive to Dominic, and that the garage business became a literal pain. The psychology of his story is that things are not intrinsically good or bad, but circumstances and coping can make them so. In Dominic's case, the physical hardship and social isolation seem to have contributed to his ordeal. His quiet, unassertive personality and conscientiousness may have led him to endure when most others would call a halt.

Sometimes our circumstances are of our own making, as in Dominic's preference for his own company at work and his generally passive coping strategies (i.e. avoiding planning actively for his retirement, accepting his lot, social isolation). As a consequence, work became a rod for his own back, leading naturally to a strong sense of relief when it was finally over. In turn, retirement was a long-awaited haven, to be gratefully enjoyed. Fortunately for Dominic, he had hobbies and friends to help him make the most of this transition, which augurs well for his successful retirement. However, it does beg questions about how his working life might have turned out had he drawn on more active coping strategies and also how this might have impacted on his retirement.

## Conclusions

To summarize this chapter, happiness is a popular, natural goal in life and retirement represents a great opportunity to achieve it through living "the good life." While health (and adequate wealth) clearly matter, it seems that we also need to take some purposeful action before we can expect to feel really happy. After all, money partly links to happiness because it is a tool with which we can work towards what we find meaning in life. Whether we are rich or poor, it is our attitude towards money that ultimately influences our happiness. Wisdom comes from living life right and so is a highway to happiness. But both share an emphasis on following a suitable process, on living by the right principles and practices, featuring a positive attitude, a sense of purpose, social giving (including compassion) and the ability to absorb oneself in whatever we are doing. That is how Dominic can rightly beam with achievement at restoring a rusty old wreck of a car.

To summarize the main points from the book's RECIPE for thriving in retirement:

Resources: Fortunately it is the sufficiency of our resources that counts most towards our happiness, so we should not feel too trapped by things like money, instead finding ways to be comfortable with what we have. What is more, there are many other resources that we need in life, so we should be thankful that much can be secured without money, such as our "social capital." It makes sense to be clear about such realities, as retirement can come as a shock to many, and will present profound challenges to us all, challenges that tend to draw heavily on our "psychological wealth" and other resources. For some this challenge is dealing with loneliness and loss, for others it is finding a fresh identity and purpose. Whatever our situation, we need to capitalize on the assets we have, working hard to improve things (e.g. enhancing social support by being sensitive, empathic, and responsive to other people's feelings). The case study of Dominic illustrates how physical and mental resources need sensitive management: Dominic ended most days feeling "extremely sore," to the point that he could hardly walk. Each working day he was "almost crippled." His situation was resolved when he took the retirement option and could avoid the hardships of his garage and thus conserve energy.

Exercise: The cliché "use it or lose it" applies to our bodies as well as to our minds, and thankfully even modest physical activity can bring health benefits and a sense of wellbeing. Exercise also opens up life enhancing experiences, including: concentrating on our actions so that we become absorbed (enjoying the feeling of being "in the zone"); participating in sport (which is like life in intense microcosm, including the pursuit of excellence); and from getting out into the elements and onto the land (a chance to feel awed by the magnificence of nature, or to get things into perspective). But, like Dominic, you also need to conserve energy, listening to your body and resting well so as to avoid exhaustion. Variety is a good way to moderate exercise, as per Ben and Katie, who mentioned a number of other activities that they had started during early retirement ... As far as Ben was concerned: "first thing I did was buy a bike ... confident there." He also took up walking ("love it ... free") and he continued to play for the company's 5-a-side football team.

Coping strategies: The book has revolved around the importance of coping, the vital business of adapting to circumstances and of seeking to shape situations to our benefit. There are 1001 ways to cope, but they can be boiled down to strategies which involve tackling stressors versus those that pivot on avoidance. Tackling stressors (e.g. loss of status or identity) adaptively features appropriate goal setting, open mindedness, a willingness to experiment (e.g. acting creatively), self-awareness, and optimizing areas of growth and counteracting areas of loss or decline. As the *learning species*, we are superbly equipped to cope with the demands of retirement and to profit from the experiences that life brings, so entering "virtuous cycles." By contrast, avoidance-based coping will tend to send us into a vicious cycle, as Trevor found when he grabbed that unexpected opportunity to retire early: Trevor found the initial 6 weeks of retirement to be a very traumatic period. He thought that he went through "denial and shock . . . a bereavement thing, including an unreal experience . . . seriously traumatic." Trevor felt that he had: "lost his identity . . . his role as an entrepreneur." But he reversed the situation successfully: To try to cope with this uncomfortable state, he drew the analogy with "having to make a new jigsaw up," one in which he represented the central pieces and where new, surrounding pieces had to be found and inserted, so that his life could form a coherent picture again. By tackling his predicament in this characteristically logical way, he was able to regain feelings of self-worth.

Intellectual activity: You should exercise your brain at every opportunity, by planning, reflecting, reframing, and so on. This can help coping by developing your self-awareness, identifying ways to continue growing, using your skills and developing more, so that we keep learning, problem-solving and developing. In turn, such coping contributes to a sense of personal control and positive self-esteem. This process contributes to wisdom, as indicated by Brian: I asked Brian whether he felt that his growing maturity had brought wisdom or contentment. He said that "Life slows down and you have more time: instead of hurrying a job you do it properly and get more satisfaction out of it." By comparison, in the past he would have thought that a job could be finished once it was "near enough" fixed. He generally gets "some satisfaction from doing things well" and smiled at the example of "beating manufacturers by repairing things that couldn't be fixed." Similarly, in addition to maintaining his commitment to the allotment, Gareth regarded it as "very important to develop new skills in the first three years after retiring, particularly attending classes in order to learn how to use a computer for email, report-writing, browsing the Internet, and so forth."

Another good intellectual habit is to try to be "positively preoccupied," relentlessly reframing what happens so that you focus on the positives, cultivating humor and other kinds of perspective. Mae provided a lovely example: Her natural tendency to reframe events positively is not limited to her interactions with customers. If the coffee machine breaks down because it's too cold then "just got to pack in, as can't make the weather . . . try not to get so frustrated . . . accept it . . . only so much you can do . . . business has its ups and downs." More generally, her basic outlook appears to be one of caring and compassion: "Everyone in life has good in them, something to give," enabling her in turn to feel good about helping them: "life's what you make it, every day." Contrast this with faulty thinking, where we take things like self-esteem away from ourselves by being illogical, unreasonable, or self-critical.

Purpose: As we manage our stressors, compensating for losses and deficits, it is especially important to find meaning, contentment, and purpose in the humdrum as well as the exceptional. Purpose can be boosted by reviewing your life and focusing on what matters to you, as well as by gaining recognition for what is done well. This can be especially difficult immediately after retiring, when you may need to find something that replaces work as the source of meaning. To be actively engaged in purposeful striving is part of the "good life." Be selective about what you attempt, nurturing and developing your interests and talents while enjoying the challenges and accomplishments. Finding a substitute for work may not be easy and can entail much trial and error, but it is vital. As captured in an earlier book on *The Psychology of Retirement*: "The best way to retire is to continue working."[19]

A key focus is on "being" rather than "having," generally moving towards harmony in your world, through a balanced and disciplined lifestyle (e.g. avoiding excesses in alcohol use and other pleasures). An outstanding instance in retirement is guiding, nurturing and mentoring others ("the crowning grace of ageing is influence."[20] Retirement came as a shock to performing arts teacher Donald, partly because he missed this part of his teaching role. When he started teaching again ... The cynicism began to evaporate, as teaching was once again fun. It was also something of profound value. Like many older adults, Donald realized afresh how important it was to contribute to the development of others ... he realized how much he could affect the development of the young teenagers in his classes, and he recognized the power of these relationships in that these youngsters "appreciate what you do." Donald now had a "real role, and a real purpose ... if I don't turn up, 120 kids will miss out."

Engagement (social support): We are profoundly social animals, needing to maintain close ties with others. Social support is informational, practical and emotional, and provides general companionship. It gives us a sense of attachment, belonging, recognition and guidance. This was indicated by grandparents John and Kate, in describing their grandson: "Frank draws us all together as a family ... for example, Frank will phone and invite us up: 'you do realize you can come and stay, any time.'" As well as "feeding us for a week," such calls help John and Kate to feel part of the community of grandparents. They have lots of family and school photos on display at home, which are a source of deep pleasure: "lovely to look at, and realize: what a lovely little fella." When together, the grandparents are accorded due authority: "When Mum's not here, you're in charge, aren't you Gran.

In closing, we should note that this psychological retirement RECIPE addresses a major and rather special transition. Unlike your earlier ones, retirement offers a golden period that starts with the end of working life. It is golden because for many it is the long-awaited opportunity to develop particular talents and interests, free from the draining demands of work. It is also golden because the time and talent are there, as never before. With resolve, ingenuity and luck, you will also find that the transition actually helps you to develop as a person and find much happiness. I do hope so. Good luck with the path ahead: *Do well and fare well.*

# Notes

## Chapter 1  The Surprises of Retirement

1. Baltes, P.B. (1997). "On the incomplete architecture of human ontogeny: Selection, optimization, and compensation as foundation of developmental theory," *American Psychologist*, 52, 366–380, p. 376.
2. M.J. Logan, M.T. Cicero [1750] *Cato Major: or his Discourse in Old Age*. Printed by S. Austen, p. 82.
3. Azar, B (2008). "Aging redefined," *Monitor on Psychology*, October, 42–3, p. 42.
4. *The Independent*, August 2008, p. 1.
5. Department of Health (2009). *New Horizons*. London: Department of Health.
6. Stirling, E. (2010). *Valuing Older People; Positive Psychological Practice*. Chichester: Wiley-Blackwell.
7. Ibid., p. 29.
8. McManus, I.C. and Furnham, A. (2010). "Fun, fun, fun: Types of fun, attitudes to fun, and their relation to personality and biographical factors," *Psychology*, 1, 159–68.
9. Ibid., p. 166.
10. Friedman, H. and Martin, L. (2011). *The Longevity Project: Surprising Discoveries for Health and Long Life from the Landmark Eight Decade Study*. London: Hay House.
11. Twenge, J.M. and Campbell, W.K. (2009). *The Narcissism Epidemic: Living in the Age of Entitlement*. London: Free Press.
12. Ibid., book cover.
13. Young, J. and Klosko, J. (1994). *Re-inventing your Life*. London: Penguin Books.
14. Mein, G., Martikainen, P., Hemingway, H., *et al.* (2003). "Is retirement good or bad for mental and physical health functioning? Whitehall II longitudinal study of civil servants," *Journal of Epidemiology & Community Health*, 57, 46–9.

*The Psychology of Retirement: Coping with the Transition from Work*, First Edition. By D. Milne.
© 2013 D. Milne. Published 2013 by John Wiley & Sons, Ltd.

15. Lazarus, R.S. and Lazarus, B.N. (2006). *Coping with Aging*. Oxford: Oxford University Press.
16. Froggatt, P. (2007). "Life after retirement," *British Medical Journal*, 335, 1323–4, p. 1323.
17. Ibid., p. 1324.
18. Ibid.
19. Ibid.

## Chapter 2   Understanding Retirement

1. Shakespeare, W. (2005). "As You Like It," *William Shakespeare: The Complete Works*. Oxford: Oxford University Press, Act 2, scene 7.
2. Vaillant, G. (1977). *Adaptation to Life*. Boston, MA: Little Brown, p. 374.
3. Shakespeare (2005), Act 2, scene 1.
4. Erikson, E.H. (1997). *The Life Cycle Completed*. New York: Norton, p. 112.
5. Ibid., p. 127.
6. Baltes, P.B. (1997). "On the incomplete architecture of human ontogeny: Selection, optimization, and compensation as foundation of developmental theory," *American Psychologist*, 52, 366–80.
7. Erikson (1997), p. 128.
8. *Concise Oxford Dictionary* (2011). "Coping," Oxford: Oxford University Press.
9. Erikson (1997), p. 4.
10. Lazarus, R.S., and Folkman, S. (1984). *Stress, Appraisal and Coping*. New York: Springer, p. 141.
11. Betancourt, I. (2010). *Even Silence Has an End*. London: Virago.
12. Ibid., p. 5.
13. Brockes, E. (2010). Fending off madness in the Columbian jungle. *The Guardian*; quotes and page numbers from the reproduced article, which appeared in *The Week* (October 2, 2010, pp. 56–7), p. 56.
14. Ibid., p.57.
15. Ibid.
16. Betancourt (2010), p. 57.
17. Ibid.
18. Pearlin, L.I. and Schooler, C. (1978). "The structure of coping," *Journal of Health and Social Behavior*, 19, 2–21.
19. Backman, L. and Hollander, B. (1991). "On the generalizability of the age-related decline in coping with high-arousal conditions in a precision sport," *Journal of Gerontology*, 46, 79–81.
20. Corneilius, S.W. and Caspi, A. (1987). "Everyday problem-solving in adulthood and old age," *Psychology & Aging*, 2, 144–53.

21. Feifal, H., Strack, S., and Nagy, V.T. (1987). "Degree of life-threat and differential use of coping modes," *Journal of Psychosomatic Research*, 31, 91–9.
22. Vaillant, G.L., Bond, M., and Vaillant, C.O. (1986). "An empirically-validated hierarchy of defence mechanisms," *Archives of General Psychiatry*, 42, 597–601.
23. Pettigrew, S. and Roberts, M. (2008). "Addressing loneliness in later life," *Aging & Mental Health*, 12, 302–9.
24. Hawkley, L.C., Hughes, M.E., Waite, L.J., *et al.* (2008). From social structural factors to perceptions of relationship quality and loneliness: The Chicago health, aging and social relations study. *Journals of Gerontology, Series B: Psychological Sciences and Social Sciences*, 63, S375–S384.
25. www.samueljohnson.com/sorrow.html (accessed May 17, 2012), para. 629.
26. De Botton, A. (2010). *The Pleasures and Sorrows of Work*. London: Penguin.
27. Ibid., p. 78.
28. Ibid., p. 106.
29. Ibid., p. 106–8.
30. Ibid., p. 182.
31. Ibid., p. 238.
32. Ibid., p. 324.
33. Ibid., p. 968.
34. *American Psychologist* (2008). Journal of The American Psychological Association, Special section on work and career, 63, 228–268.
35. Ibid., p. 230.
36. Zhan, Y., Wang, M., Liu, S., *et al.* (2009). "Bridge employment and retirees' health: A longitudinal investigation," *Journal of Occupational Health Psychology*, 14, 374–89.
37. Sutton, J. (2011). "Life's long and winding road," *The Psychologist*, 24, 748–50.
38. Froggatt, P. (2007). "Life after retirement," *British Medical Journal*, 335, 1323–4, p. 1324.
39. Ibid.
40. This quotation is often attributed to Darwin. It is believed to have been originally said by Clarence Darrow, as quoted in *Improving the Quality of Life for the Black Elderly: Challenges and Opportunities: Hearing before the Select Committee on Aging, House of Representatives, One Hundredth Congress, first session, September 25, 1987* (1988).

## Chapter 3 Reframing Retirement

1. See www.quotationspage.com (accessed May 21, 2012).
2. Finn, S. (2011). "A dream childhood and an inspiring adult," *The Northumbrian, Winter Edition*, 31–3.
3. Facey, A. (1981). *A Fortunate Life*. New York: Penguin.

4. Ibid., p. 320.
5. Ibid., p. 323.
6. Karp, D.A. (1989). "The social construction of retirement among professionals 50–60 years old," *The Gerontologist*, 29, 750–60.
7. Hildon, Z., Smith, G., Netuveli, G., and Blane, D. (2008). "Understanding adversity and resilience at older ages," *Sociology of Health & Illness*, 30, 726–40.
8. Ibid., p. 732.
9. Ibid., p. 738.
10. Janoff-Bulman, R. (1989). "Assumptive worlds and the stress of traumatic events: Application of the schema construct," *Social Cognition*, 7, 113–36.
11. Thouless, R.H. (1930). *Straight and Crooked Thinking*. London: Pan Books.
12. Ibid., p. 39.
13. Ibid., p. 171.
14. Ibid.
15. Ibid., p. 172.
16. Ibid., p. 173.
17. Ibid., p. 175.
18. Butler, G. and Hope, T. (1995). *Manage Your Mind*. Oxford: Oxford University Press.
19. Micah 6:8. New International Version.
20. Richardson, F.C., Fowers, B.J., and Guignon (Eds) (1999). *Re-envisioning Psychology*. San Francisco: Jossey-Bass, p. 31.
21. Nozick, R. (1989). *The Examined Life*. New York: Simon & Schuster.
22. Mark 8:36. Authorized King James Version.
23. John Ruskin (1881). Essay IV "Ad Valorem," in *Unto this Last*. New York: Wiley, p. 135.
24. Cited at: http://blog.talkingphilosophy.com/?p=1307
25. Ecclesiastes 9:11. New Living Translation.
26. Quoted in *The Daily Telegraph*; cited in *The Week*, December 10, 2011, p. 25.
27. Schopenhauer, A. (1844). "On the Road to Salvation," *The World as Will and Idea*, Leipzig.
28. Orlick, T. (2008). *In Pursuit of Excellence*. Champaign, IL: Human Kinetics.
29. Ibid., pp. 13–14.
30. See www.worldofquotes.com/author/Woody+Allen/3/index.html (accessed May 21, 2012).

## Chapter 4  Relating in Retirement

1. Aronson, E. (2008). *The Social Animal* (10th edn). New York: Worth/Freeman.
2. Macaskill, M. (2010). "Broken hearts are a real killer." *The Sunday Times*, November 14, p. 19.

3. Lavallee, D. (2005). The effect of life development intervention on sports careers transition adjustment. *The Sports Psychologist*, 19, 193–202.
4. "Life after the White House," *The Week*, January 24, 2009, p. 13.
5. Ibid.
6. Nahum-Shani, I. and Bamberger, P.A. (2009). "Work hours, retirement and supportive relations among older adults," *Journal of Organizational Behaviour*, 30, 1–25.
7. Van Solinge, H. and Henkens, K. (2005). "Couples' adjustment to retirement: A multi-actor panel study," *Journal of Gerontology, Social Sciences*, 60B, S11–S20.
8. Ibid., p. S17.
9. Hildon, Z., Smith, G., Netuveli, G., *et al.* (2008). "Understanding adversity and resilience at older ages," *Sociology of Health & Illness*, 30, 726–40.
10. Harris, T.J.R., Pistrang, N., and Barker, C. (2006). "Couples' experiences of the support process in depression: A phenomenological analysis," *Psychology and Psychotherapy: Theory, Research & Practice*, 79, 1–21.
11. Ibid., p. 13.
12. Smith, P.K. and Drew, L.M. (2002). "Grandparenthood," in M. Bornstein (Ed.) *Handbook of Parenting*. Vol. 3. Mahwah, NJ: Lawrence Erlbaum, pp. 141–72.
13. "Grandparents Plus" (2009). Policy briefing paper (www.grandparents.org.uk).
14. Ibid.
15. Ibid.
16. Smith, P.K. (2005). "Grandparents and grandchildren," *The Psychologist*, 18, 684–7.
17. Ibid., p. 685.
18. Smith and Drew (2002), pp. 141–72.
19. Smith (2005), p. 684.
20. "Grandparents Plus" (2009).
21. Adfam (2006). *Forgotten Families*. London: Adfam.
22. Ibid.
23. Ibid.
24. Ibid., p. 2.
25. Reitzes, D.C. and Mutran, E.J. (2004). "Grandparenthood: Factors influencing frequency of grandparent–grandchildren contact and grandparent role satisfaction," *Journal of Gerontology*, 59B, S9–S16.
26. Ibid.
27. Study conducted by myself and Catherine Brew cited in Milne, D. (1999). *Social Therapy*. New York: Wiley, pp. 174–6.
28. Ibid.
29. Archer, J. and Winchester, G. (1994). "Bereavement following death of a pet," *British Journal of Psychology*, 85, 259–71.
30. Wells, D. (2011). "The value of pets for human health," *The Psychologist*, 24, 172–6.

31. Ibid., p. 172.
32. Reitzes and Mutran (2004), pp. 172–3.

## Chapter 5  Supporting Retirement

1. Morgan, G.S., Wisneski, D.C., and Skitka, L.J. (2011). "The expulsion from Disneyland," *American Psychologist*, 66, 447–54.
2. Kipling, R. "The English Flag," stanza 1, http://en.wikisource.org/wiki/The_English_Flag (accessed May 23, 2012).
3. Milne, D. (1999). *Social Therapy*. Chichester: Wiley.
4. Reid, J. (1972). *Alienation.* Rectoral address, Glasgow University.
5. Ibid.
6. Ibid.
7. See www.census.gov/population/www/socdemo/age/ (accessed May 25, 2012).
8. Ibid.
9. Lyon, R. (2011). "Letter to *The Independent*," cited in *The Week*, January 22, 2011, p. 23.
10. Devine-Wright, P. (2009). "Rethinking NIMBYism: The role of place attachment and place identity in explaining place-protective action," *Journal of Community & Applied Social Psychology*, 19, 426–41.
11. Ibid.
12. Morgan, Wisneski, and Skitka (2011).
13. Ibid.
14. Liu, L. (2008). "To have and to be: Towards the social representation of quality of life in China," *Journal of Community & Applied Social Psychology*, 18, 233–52.
15. Ibid., p. 242.
16. Nimrod, G., and Rotem, A. (2010). "Between relaxation and excitement: Activities and benefits gained in retirees' tourism," *International Journal of Tourism Research*, 12, 65–78.
17. Jarrett, C. (2011). "Wish you were here?" *The Psychologist*, 24, 574–8.
18. Ibid.
19. Fu-Chen, C. and Wu, C-C. (2009). "How motivations, constraints and demographic factors predict seniors' overseas travel propensity," *Asia Pacific Management Review*, 14, 301–12.
20. Vingerhoets, A.J.J.M., Huijgevoort, M., and Van Heck, G.L. (2002). "Leisure sickness: A pilot study on its prevalence, phenomenology and background," *Psychotherapy & Psychosomatics*, 71, 311–17.
21. Jarrett (2011).
22. Caserta, M., Lund, D., Utz, R., and de Vries, B. (2009). "Stress-related growth among the recently bereaved," *Aging and Mental Health*, 13, 463–76.

23. Dawkins, R. (2006). *The God Delusion*. Boston: Houghton Mifflin.
24. Collicut, J. (2011). "Psychology, religion, and spirituality," *The Psychologist*, 24, 250–1.
25. De Botton, A. (2012). *Religion for Atheists*. London: Penguin.
26. Ibid., p. 12

# Chapter 6  Learning from Life

1. Hein, P. (1966). *Grooks*. Copenhagen: Borgen.
2. Kolb, D.A. (1984). *Experiential Learning*. Englewood Cliffs, NJ: Prentice-Hall.
3. Dewey, J. (1910). *How We Think*. New York: Prometheus Books.
4. Bolt, C. (2000). *The Book of Answers*. London: Bantam Books.
5. Morrison, M. and Roese, N.J. (2011). "Regrets of the typical American: Findings from a nationally-representative sample," *Social Psychological & Personality Science*, 2, 576–83.
6. Ibid.
7. Ibid., p. 580.
8. Ibid., p. 581.
9. Butler, G., and Hope, T. (2007). *Manage Your Mind: The Mental Fitness Guide*. Oxford: Oxford University Press.
10. Gray, S., Cited in *The Week*, April 16, 2011, p. 21.
11. Allen, Woody (1975). *Without Feathers*. New York: Random House.
12. Caresse, J.A., Mullaney, J.L., Faden, R.R., and Finucane, T.E. (2002). "Planning for death but not serious future illness: qualitative study of housebound elderly patients," *British Medical Journal*, 325, 125–37.
13. Ibid., 125.
14. Firestone, R.W. and Catlett, J. (2000). *Fear of Intimacy*. Washington, DC: American Psychological Association.
15. Kubler-Ross, E. (1969). *On Death and Dying*. London: Routledge.
16. Kolb (1984).
17. Placido Domingo, *The Independent*: www.independent.co.uk/arts-entertainment/classical/features/placido-domingo-if-i-rest-i-rust-2009618.html (accessed May 23, 2012).
18. Cited in *The Week*, February 26, 2011, p. 12.
19. Cited in *The Week*, September 18, 2010, p. 21.
20. Lund, D., Caserta, M., Utz, R., *et al.* (2010). "Experiences and early coping of bereaved spouses/partners in an intervention based on the dual-process model," *Omega (Westport)*, 61, 291–313, p. 2.
21. Waller, N.G., Putnam, F.W., and Carlson, E.B. (1996). "Types of dissociation and dissociative types: A taxometric analysis of dissociative experiences," *Psychological Methods*, 1(3), 300–21.

## Chapter 7   Learning for Life

1. Cited by Diamond, M. (2001). "Successful aging of the healthy brain." Paper presented at *The Conference of the American Society on Aging*, March 10, Chicago.
2. Ibid.
3. Tilbrook, H.E., Cox, H., Hewitt, C.E., *et al.* (2011). "Yoga for chronic low back pain," *Annals of Internal Medicine*, 155, 569–78.
4. Karel, M.J., Gatz, M., and Smyer, M.A. (2012). "Aging and mental health in the decade ahead." *American Psychologist*, 67, 184–98, p. 191.
5. National Alzheimer's Association (2011). *Facts and Figures.* Chicago: Alzheimer's Association.
6. Karel, Gatz, and Smyer, (2012).
7. Gallwey, W.T. (1979). *The Inner Game of Golf.* London: Pan Books, p. 97.
8. De Botton, A. (2002). *The Art of Travel.* London: Penguin, p. 20.
9. Ibid., p. 122.
10. Ibid., p. 113.
11. Ibid., p. 9.
12. Ibid., p. 243.
13. Gallwey (1979).
14. Jane Maher cited in *The Week*, August 20, 2011, p.17.
15. *The Week*, August 20, 2011, p. 17.
16. Wilkinson, J.. (2011). *Jonny: My Autobiography.* London: Headline.
17. Blake, W (2011). "Augeries of Innocence," *The Poems of William Blake.* London: Createspace.
18. Gallwey (1979), p. 228.
19. Rotella, B. (2004). *Golf is not a Game of Perfect.* London: Pocket Books, p. 29.
20. Dewey (1910).
21. Stathopoulou, G., Powers, M.B., Berry, A.C., *et al.* (2006). "Exercise interventions for mental health: A quantitative and qualitative review," *Clinical Psychology: Science and Practice*, 13, 179–93.
22. Hope, J. (2008). "Jogging or cycling through middle age 'can delay ageing by 12 years'." *Mail* online, www.dailymail.co.uk/health/article-558499/Jogging-cycling-middle-age-delay-ageing-12-years.html (accessed May 23, 2012).
23. National Statistics (2008). *Health Survey for England 2006.* Landon: National Health Service.
24. *USA Today* March 17, 2010.
25. Hamer, M., Stamatakis, E., and Steptoe, A. (2009). "Dose-response relationship between physical activity and mental health: the Scottish Health Survey," *British Journal of Sports Medicine*, 43, 111–14.
26. Cited in *The Week*, October 20, 2011, p. 21.
27. Wen, C.P., Wai, J.P.M., Tsai, M.K., *et al.* (2011). "Minimum amount of physical activity for reduced mortality and extended life expectancy: a prospective cohort study," *The Lancet*, doi: 10.1016/SO140-6736 (11) 60749-6.

28. Diamond (2001).
29. Renaud, M., Maquestiaux, F., Joncas, S., *et al.* (2010). "The effect of three months of aerobic training on response preparation in older adults," *Frontiers in Aging Neuroscience*, 2, 1–9.
30. Nazimek, J. (2009). "Active body, healthy mind," *The Psychologist*, 22, 206–8.
31. Ibid., 207.
32. As summarized in: Smyth, C. (2011). "Nearly half of all cancer cases could be wiped out with healthier lifestyles," *The Times*, December 7, p. 5.
33. Ibid.

## Chapter 8  Conclusions

1. Baron de Montesquieu cited in *The Week*, April 9, 2011, p. 19.
2. Andrew Grice (2010). "Prime Minister unveils 'happiness index'," *The Independent*, November 20.
3. Nozick, R. (2006). *The Examined Life*. New York: Simon & Schuster.
4. Ibid., p. 113.
5. Rosemary Bennett (2012). "Male, 45, divorced and in London? You may be Britain's most miserable person," *The Times*, February 29, p. 4.
6. Cited in *The Week*, April 30, 2011, p. 18.
7. Jones, J.M., Haslam, S.A., Jetten, J., *et al.* (2011). "That which doesn't kill us can make us stronger (and more satisfied with life): The contribution of personal and social changes to well-being after acquired brain injury," *Psychology and Health*, 26, 353–69.
8. De Botton (2010), p. 96.
9. Diener, E., and Biswas-Diener, R. (2008). *Happiness: Unlocking the Mysteries of Psychological Wealth*. Oxford: Blackwell, pp. 91–111, 240–1.
10. Cited in Firestone, R.W. and Catlett, J. (2009). *Beyond Death Anxiety*. New York: Springer.
11. Sutton, J. (2011). "Life's long and winding road," *The Psychologist*, 24, 748–50, p. 748.
12. Killingsworth, M.A. and Gilbert, D.T. (2010). "A wandering mind is an unhappy mind," *Science*, 330, 932–4.
13. Ibid., p. 394.
14. Diener and Biswas-Diener (2008).
15. Fischer, R. and Boer, D. (2011). "What Is more important for national well-being: Money or autonomy? A Meta-analysis of well-being, burnout, and anxiety across 63 societies," *Journal of Personality & Social Psychology*, 101, 164–84.
16. Diener and Biswas-Diener (2008), p. 230.
17. Grossmann, I., Na, J., Varnum, M.E.W., *et al.* (2010). "Reasoning about social conflicts improves into old age," *Proceedings of the National Academy of Sciences of the USA*, 107, 7246–50.

18. Lao Tsu (1973). *Tao Te Ching* [The Way]. London: Wildwood House, verse 9.
19. The Everyday Psychologist (1999). *The Psychology of Retirement* (Arlington Heights, IL: Business Psychology Research Institute), p. 29.
20. Cicero, M.T. (2002). *On Old Age (De Senectute)*. Wauconda, IL: Bolchzy-Carducci.

# Recommended Reading

## Recommended Reading

Bolt, C. (2000). *The Book of Answers.* London: Bantam.

Bransford, J.D., Brown, A.L., and Cocking, R.R. (2000). *How People Learn.* Washington, DC: National Research Council.

Burns, D.D. (1981). *Feeling Good: The New Mood Therapy.* New York: Penguin.

Butler, G., and Hope, T. (2007). *Manage Your Mind.* Oxford: Oxford University Press.

De Botton, A. (2002). *The Art of Travel.* London: Penguin.

Diener, E., and Biswas-Diener, R. (2008). *Happiness: Unlocking the Mysteries of Psychological Wealth.* Oxford: Blackwell.

Erikson, E.H. (1997). *The Life Cycle Completed.* New York: Norton.

Firestone, R.W., and Catlett, J. (2009). *Beyond Death Anxiety.* New York: Springer.

Friedman, H., and Martin, L. (2011). *The Longevity Project: Surprising Discoveries for Health and Long Life from the Landmark Eight Decade Study.* London: Hay House.

Gallwey, W.T., Hazelik, E.S., and Horton, J. (2009). *The Inner Game of Stress: Outsmart Life's Challenges and Fullfil Your Potential.* New York: Random House.

Hagland, C. (2011). *Happy Retirement.* Oxford: One World.

Lazarus, R.S., and Lazarus, B.N. (2006). *Coping with Aging.* Oxford: Oxford University Press.

Longhurst, M. (2000). *The Beginner's Guide to Retirement.* Dublin: Newleaf.

Milne, D.L. (2004). *Coping with a Mid-Life Crisis.* London: Sheldon Books.

Orlick, T. (2008). *In Pursuit of Excellence: How to Win in Sport and Life Through Mental Training* (4th edn). Leeds: Human Kinetics.

*The Psychology of Retirement: Coping with the Transition from Work,* First Edition. By D. Milne.
© 2013 D. Milne. Published 2013 by John Wiley & Sons, Ltd.

Smith, P.K., and Drew, L.M. (2003). "Grand-parenting and extended support networks," in: M. Hoghughi and N. Long, (Eds) *Handbook of Parenting*. London: Sage, pp. 146–59.

Stirling, E. (2010). *Valuing Older People; Positive Psychological Practice*. Chichester: Wiley-Blackwell.

Sutton, J. (2011). "Life's long and winding road," *The Psychologist*, 24, 748–50.

Twenge, J.M., and Campbell, W.K. (2009). *The Narcissism Epidemic: Living in the Age of Entitlement*. London: Free Press.

WHICH? (2003). *Guide to Making the Most of Your Retirement*. London: Consumers Association.

Young, J., and Klosko, J. (1994). *Re-inventing Your Life*. London: Penguin Books.

# Index